WILDLIVES

50 EXTRAORDINARY ANIMALS
THAT MADE HISTORY

Atheneum Books for Young Readers

NEW YORK LONDON TORONTO SYDNEY NEW DELHI

FOR JOSEPH AND BETHAN
—B. L.

TO FIONA AND WOLFIE, A LOVABLE CAT LOAF AND A SCRAPPY PUP. AND FOR COLIN, FOR TAKING SUCH GOOD CARE OF THEM. AND US . . .
—S. W.

ATHENEUM BOOKS FOR YOUNG READERS
An imprint of Simon & Schuster Children's Publishing Division
1230 Avenue of the Americas, New York, New York 10020
Text copyright © 2019 by Ben Lerwill
Illustrations copyright © 2019 by Sarah Walsh
Originally published in Great Britain by Nosy Crow Ltd.
For a full list of photo credits, see page 111.
All rights reserved, including the right of reproduction in whole or in part in any form.
ATHENEUM BOOKS FOR YOUNG READERS is a registered trademark of Simon & Schuster, Inc.
Atheneum logo is a trademark of Simon & Schuster, Inc.
For information about special discounts for bulk purchases, please contact Simon & Schuster
Special Sales at 1-866-506-1949 or business@simonandschuster.com.
The Simon & Schuster Speakers Bureau can bring authors to your live event. For more information
or to book an event, contact the Simon & Schuster Speakers Bureau at 1-866-248-3049
or visit our website at www.simonspeakers.com.
The text for this book was set in Filson Soft.
The illustrations for this book were rendered in gouache, colored pencil, and Photoshop.
Manufactured in China
1119 SCP
First Atheneum Books for Young Readers Edition February 2020
2 4 6 8 10 9 7 5 3 1
Library of Congress Cataloging-in-Publication Data
Names: Lerwill, Ben, author. | Walsh, Sarah, illustrator.
Title: Wildlives : 50 extraordinary animals that made history / Ben Lerwill, Sarah Walsh.
Description: First edition. | New York, New York : Atheneum Books for Young Readers, [2020] | Includes
index. | Audience: Ages 8 and Up | Audience: Grades 4–6 | Summary: "We often read heroic stories of
brave people who made their mark on history. But did you know there are some pretty courageous
creatures in our world, too? This captivating collection gathers fifty heartwarming, surprising,
and powerful true stories of animals around the world who displayed immense bravery, aided in
groundbreaking discoveries, and showed true friendship. Featuring a range of animals-from heroes
to helpers, adventurers to achievers, and many more-young readers will discover some of the most
unforgettable animals of all time. Compelling and gorgeously illustrated, *WildLives* is the perfect
introduction to some of the amazing animals whose wild lives have made history"— Provided by publisher.
Identifiers: LCCN 2019031856 | ISBN 9781534454842 (hardcover) | ISBN 9781534454859 (eBook)
Subjects: LCSH: Animals—Anecdotes—Juvenile literature.
Classification: LCC QL791 .L635 2020 | DDC 590—dc23
LC record available at https://lccn.loc.gov/2019031856

CONTENTS

IT SEEMS TO ME THAT THE NATURAL WORLD IS THE GREATEST SOURCE OF EXCITEMENT ... IT IS THE GREATEST SOURCE OF SO MUCH IN LIFE THAT MAKES LIFE WORTH LIVING.

 —Sir David Attenborough

INTRODUCTION

What jumps into your mind when you think about the animal kingdom? It might be a lion prowling across the savannah. It might be a whale diving in the deep. It might be a puppy curled up on your lap or an eagle soaring over the mountains. It might be a fox or a frog, a baboon or a bear, a tiny turtle or a terrifying tiger. Nature is full of incredible creatures, and we're unbelievably lucky to share our planet with them all. Animals are amazing.

There are more than a million recorded animal species in the world, from the smallest tiddlers in the shallows to the biggest beasts in the jungle. Every single one of them is fascinating, but sometimes we hear about animals that have lived extra-special lives. Animals that have made important discoveries, taught us more about the world, or even saved the lives of others. Animals that have made history.

This book is a celebration of some of the most famous and unforgettable animals of all time, and the remarkable lives that they've lived. The 50 stories here are all true. Some of them might make you laugh. Some of them might make you stop and think. All of them will help you to see just how brave, clever, and fantastic animals can be.

Of course, despite the title of this book, not all animals live in the wild. Many live at home with humans, while others live on farms, in zoos, or in other man-made places. Many of the animals included here have done incredible things despite having very little choice about how and where they lived. In lots of ways, it makes their achievements and adventures even more astonishing.

There are 50 history-making stories in this book, but there could easily have been 500. They tell the tales of small animals and tall animals, animals that swim and animals that fly, animals that we see every day and animals that are much rarer. All of them, however, deserve to have their life stories told here. So, the next time you're admiring one of nature's courageous creatures, make sure you remind yourself that wild lives are often wonderful lives—because animals can do truly extraordinary things.

CHER AMI

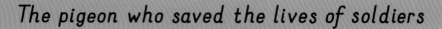
The pigeon who saved the lives of soldiers

FLY AWAY HOME

War heroes don't often have wings. When we talk about bravery in battle, we usually think of people who have risked their lives to help others. We don't often think of birds, which is why the tale of Cher Ami is so extraordinary. In 1918 in France, during the First World War, the little pigeon managed to save almost 200 lives.

Homing pigeons like Cher Ami are incredible birds. Each one learns to know where its home is, and will return there even when that home is many, many miles away. For this reason, homing pigeons—also called carrier pigeons—have been used for hundreds of years to send messages across long distances, with small notes attached to their legs.

PIGEON MESSAGE

October 4th 1918
To: 308th Infantry
From: Major Charles Whittlesey

We are along the road paralell 276.4.
Our artillery is dropping a barrage directly on us.
For heavens sake **stop** it.

The message Cher Ami carried for many miles.

BRAVERY IN BATTLE

In the First World War, the United States Army used more than 600 birds to carry messages across the battlefields of France. None of them was quite as heroic as Cher Ami. She had already delivered more than ten important messages during the war, but her final mission was her most famous.

On October 4, 1918, she came to the rescue when a battalion of American soldiers found themselves in a very dangerous situation. The soldiers, led by Major Charles Whittlesey, were being fired at by both the enemy and their own side, who didn't realize they were there. They needed to get a message out to stop the attack—and fast. The major wrote a note that read: "We are along the road parallel 276.4. Our artillery is dropping a barrage directly on us. For heaven's sake stop it." It was tied to the leg of Cher Ami, and while bombs and bullets whistled through the air, the bird rose into the sky.

Cher Ami was awarded the Croix de Guerre medal for bravery.

The enemy knew exactly what was happening and shot at Cher Ami. She was hit almost immediately, in the breast, leg, and eye, and fell to the ground. But her injuries weren't enough to stop her. Amazingly, she took off again, flapping upward through another storm of bullets and flying 25 miles in less than half an hour to reach her base. She arrived blinded in one eye and coated in blood, but her message was still dangling from her wounded leg.

Orders were given to stop the attack straightaway, and 194 of the American soldiers that had been surrounded were rescued. Cher Ami means "dear friend" in French, so the bird's name was a very good one—she was celebrated as a hero. The medics at the base made her a wooden leg to replace the one that had been shot, and she was given the French Croix de Guerre, a war medal.

MAKING HISTORY

Whole books have been written about Cher Ami. Her story has even appeared in films. After the war, she returned to America by boat and was made part of the Racing Pigeon Hall of Fame. Her one-legged body is still on display at the National Museum of American History in Washington, DC. It's a fitting way to remember a very determined bird and the long, courageous flight she made while the battle raged around her.

66 *So with the message tied on tight,*
I flew up straight with all my might;
Before I got up high enough,
Those watchful guns began to puff.

Machine-gun bullets came like rain,
You'd think I was an airplane;
And when I started to the rear,
My! the shot was coming near!

But on I flew, straight as a bee,
The wind could not catch up with me. 99

—excerpt from the poem "Cher Ami," by Harry Webb Farrington

SIMON

CATCHING RATS AND SAILORS' HATS

Sometimes, small animals can make a big difference. You might not think a cat could ever help the sailors of a huge British warship, but that's exactly what one little black-and-white cat did. It was 1948 when the ship, HMS *Amethyst*, sailed into the Asian port of Hong Kong. Here, among the city's colorful temples and noisy markets, a 17-year-old sailor named George Hickinbottom found a tiny, hungry cat on the dockside. This is how Simon's story began.

George decided to look after the thin, young cat. He hid Simon under his clothes and smuggled him onto the ship, then made a place in his cabin for him to rest. George was worried about what the ship's captain would say once he saw the cat. But when Captain Griffiths noticed Simon, he was happy rather than angry. The ship needed a cat to help get rid of all the rats that had got on board. Rats can spread germs and damage food supplies—and the sailors soon learned that Simon was a very good ratcatcher indeed.

He chased the rats everywhere, scampering across the decks and pouncing under tables, covering the ship from top to bottom. When he trapped a rat—which was often—he liked to carry the body in his mouth and lay it at the captain's feet. Sometimes he even left dead rats on the captain's bed! And when the captain took his hat off, Simon loved curling up inside his gold-braided cap. He was becoming a popular part of the ship's crew.

DANGER ON THE RIVER

The other sailors adored having Simon around. He boosted their morale, which means he made them feel happier about life at sea. Even when George and Captain Griffiths had to leave the ship, Simon stayed on board. The new captain, Captain Skinner, quickly became fond of the playful cat. But one day, while sailing up the hot, winding Yangtze River in China, Simon's ship found itself in big trouble.

It was 1949 and a time of war in China. Suddenly, from the green mountains on either side of the river, there came missiles and gunshots. The fighters on the shore thought HMS *Amethyst* was an enemy boat. The ship was very badly damaged. Many sailors died, including Captain Skinner, and lots more were hurt. Simon had nasty injuries on his back and his legs, and when some sailors found him, he was tired, burned, and weak. But the ship's doctor helped him to get better.

Simon with the crewmen of HMS *Amethyst*.

The ship was still in a lot of danger. It wasn't safe to sail back down the river, so it became trapped where it was. But slowly, bravely, Simon returned to his normal life on board. He caught rats, patrolled the decks, and sat on the beds of the injured sailors, helping to keep their spirits up in what was a very scary situation.

> 66 *Simon's company and expertise as a ratcatcher were invaluable during the months we were held captive. During a terrifying time, he helped boost the morale of many young sailors.* 99
> —ship's lieutenant Stewart Hett, who was appointed "cat officer"

MAKING HISTORY

It took more than 100 days for HMS *Amethyst* to escape the heat and gunfire of the Yangtze River. Everyone on board had to survive on very little food and water. When the ship finally reached the safety of the sea, the crew members were treated as heroes. Simon was given the Dickin Medal, a special award for animals who do great things in wartime. Even today, he is still the only cat to ever receive this honor.

Simon's life was short, and not easy. He lived for only a few more weeks after arriving in England and was buried at a cemetery in London. The stone above his grave is a fine tribute to a very faithful cat. It reads in part: "In memory of Simon. Awarded Dickin Medal August 1949. Throughout the Yangtze Incident his behavior was of the highest order."

9

WOJTEK

The bear who became a soldier

FROM CUB TO CAMPMATE

During the Second World War, the Polish Army had one soldier who was different from all the rest. He had four legs, sharp claws, and shaggy brown fur. His name was Wojtek (pronounced Voy-tek), and he was a bear who lived a very unexpected life. His story is incredible, although if he hadn't been spotted on the roadside as a cub, he might never have had much of a story at all.

In April 1942 thousands of Polish soldiers were being taken from Russia to the Middle East. One day, as they were passing through Persia—a country now called Iran—they met a young boy holding a sack. Inside was a tiny bear cub. Its mother had been shot by hunters in the hills, and the cub looked thin and frightened.

The soldiers decided to buy the bear from the boy and look after it themselves. So they traded some money, a penknife, some chocolate, and a tin of beef for the boy's sack with the orphan cub inside. But do you think, on that day, any of them ever imagined that the little bear would grow up to become a soldier?

> **" He loved to drink from a beer bottle, and when it was empty, he would look through the opening to see where the rest of the beer was. "**
> —Dymitr Szawlugo, a Polish soldier

> **" He had a pay book. He didn't receive money, but was officially a Polish soldier. I felt like he was my older brother. "**
> —Wojciech Narebski, a Polish soldier

The men called him Wojtek, which means "happy warrior," and they began to feed him. They gave him milk and kept him warm at night by wrapping him in a big army coat. By the time they reached their next camp, the bear was already growing fast. He liked jumping in and out of the army trucks and trying to climb trees. The commanding officer noticed that lots of the soldiers were much happier when Wojtek was around.

As the Polish soldiers traveled around the Middle East, they kept Wojtek with them and he soon became part of the family. He was given double rations, which means he had twice as much to eat as the soldiers. Like all bears, he loved eating fruit and honey, but he also liked drinking beer when it was given to him! Wojtek enjoyed play-wrestling with the men, and at night he sometimes even slept in their tents. But the bear often got into mischief, too—he kept cool by turning on the showers when he wasn't allowed to, and once he even pulled a load of underwear from the camp washing line!

A BEAR IN BATTLE

Then the war meant that the soldiers had to sail to Italy. They wanted to take Wojtek with them, but for him to be allowed on the ship, he had to have special permission from the leaders of the army. They decided that the brown bear did such a good job of cheering up the men that this would be a great idea. So, on February 13, 1944, the ship set sail from Egypt carrying Poland's newest soldier: "Private Wojtek," who now weighed around 440 pounds and could stand more than six feet tall.

He would have been a very scary sight on the battlefield—and unbelievably, three months later, that's exactly where he was. At the Battle of Monte Cassino in Italy, where the Polish soldiers fought against the Germans, Wojtek helped by carrying heavy boxes of bullets and bombs while standing upright! The noise and panic of the battle would have been terrifying and very confusing for a bear, but he stayed close to his human friends and survived.

Wojtek playing with troops (*above*) and the badge of the Second Polish Corps, showing Wojtek carrying a bomb (*right*).

MAKING HISTORY

When people found out about Wojtek's bravery in battle, he became a hero. The Polish soldiers had a special logo made that showed a bear carrying a bomb. He appeared on television and had many books written about him. After the war, he was taken to Scotland, along with some of the Polish soldiers, and he spent the rest of his life in Edinburgh Zoo. Wojtek had never been able to live the normal life of a bear, but his story will never be forgotten. During a dangerous war, he made an enormous difference to the people who knew him.

MOKO

The dolphin who rescued two stranded whales

OUT OF THE ORDINARY

Dolphins are some of the most impressive animals on the planet. They swim quickly, learn quickly, and think quickly—and if you've ever been lucky enough to watch them darting and diving through the waves, you'll know that they're agile, playful, and speedy. They give us lots of reasons to admire them, but one very clever dolphin gave us even more reasons than most. He lived in the waters off New Zealand, and his name was Moko.

In 2007 the people living around Mahia Beach, on New Zealand's North Island, began to notice a young bottlenose dolphin in the bay. Unusually, he came back to the same place every few days and always seemed to be on his own, but he felt comfortable enough to approach people in the water. Soon the lively dolphin—which they named Moko, after the nearby headland of Mokotahi—had become a local celebrity.

Moko was named after Mokotahi, near the blue seas of the Mahia Peninsula.

> 66 *The way that Moko interacted with people really inspired public interest and care for dolphins and marine mammals and their environment.* 99
>
> —Andrew Baucke, a local conservationist

Moko would swim right up to boats, twist calmly through groups of swimmers, and push kayaks through the water with his nose. Sometimes he could even be quite cheeky—stealing paddles and tipping over water-skiers! It wasn't unusual to see a dolphin here—the seas in the area have always been full of amazing marine life—but it was very rare to see a wild animal behaving like this. Scientists thought Moko must have become lost from the rest of his pod and decided to make the bay his home. He still went swimming in the deeper waters farther offshore, but he always came back.

12

PELORUS JACK

Moko wasn't the first New Zealand dolphin to act as an important guide. Between 1888 and 1912, a Risso's dolphin named Pelorus Jack became famous for leading boats through a dangerously narrow stretch of water in the Marlborough Sounds, on New Zealand's South Island. He helped boats by swimming next to them for an amazing 24 years.

Famous Pelorus Jack guiding ships through the water.

> *Moko just came flying through the water and pushed in between us and the whales. He got them to head toward the hill, where the channel is. It was an amazing experience.*
>
> —Juanita Symes, one of the people on the beach

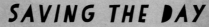

SAVING THE DAY

Then one day in 2008, the people around the beach became very worried. Two pygmy sperm whales, a mother and her calf, had gotten lost and become stranded on the sand. They were scared and very confused, because they didn't understand which way they needed to turn in the shallow water. As people tried to help them, the whales got more and more frightened, calling out to each other with whistles and clicks. It was looking like the poor whales would die if they couldn't get back to deeper water soon. Then a familiar dolphin swam into the bay.

Moko understood straightaway that the whales were in danger. The people watching say that he seemed to communicate with the mother and her calf, and that almost immediately the whales stopped panicking. Instead they followed Moko as he led them back along the shoreline, through a narrow channel, and back into the wide-open sea. The whales were safe—and Moko was a hero.

MAKING HISTORY

Moko lived for just two more years, and his kindness, intelligence, and spirit have never been forgotten. People have known for a long time that dolphins can do very thoughtful things for each other, for humans, and for other animals, and Moko showed us just how caring they can be.

NING NONG

The elephant who saved a girl from drowning

LIFE ON THE BEACH

Sometimes animals can see, hear, or smell things that humans can't. Sometimes they notice things a long time before we do, in ways that we don't quite understand. This is what happened on a beach in Thailand one morning in 2004, when a young elephant found himself in a terrifying situation. A huge, unstoppable wave, known as a tidal wave or tsunami, was on its way. But when the elephant realized the danger he was in, he had someone else to think about too: the schoolgirl who was riding on his back!

The elephant's name was Ning Nong, and he was just four years old. He was small but strong, with a dark gray trunk, flapping ears, and sturdy legs. He lived on the island of Phuket in Thailand, which is where he was on December 26, the day after Christmas. The weather was sunny and the beach was full of tourists. One of them was an eight-year-old girl from England named Amber Owen, who was on vacation with her family.

Like some other elephants, Ning Nong had to work on the beach, giving people rides along the sand. Amber liked him a lot. She fed him bananas every day and always made sure it was Ning Nong that carried her when she went for a ride. But on this morning, after Amber climbed onto his back, the little elephant started acting strangely.

WARNING SIGNS

He normally walked quietly along the shore, but today he got very anxious, pulling away from the water and trying to hurry away from the beach. The mahout, or elephant handler, didn't understand what Ning Nong was doing, and neither did Amber. Then people noticed something unusual. The tide was rushing out very quickly, as if the seawater was being sucked back into the ocean. What was going on?

> **" He knew something was wrong and began running as fast as he could inland. "**
> —Amber Owen, the girl rescued by Ning Nong

It was a warning that a tsunami was coming. When it arrived, it hit the beach with such force that whole buildings were destroyed. Many people got caught in the powerful, crashing waters. Ning Nong, however, had had a head start. He had understood very early that something was wrong and had run inland, with a frightened Amber clinging on tight. But despite the elephant's quick thinking, they were still in a lot of danger. The enormous wave didn't stop at the beach. It roared up behind them, and soon the water came up to Ning Nong's shoulders!

> " *He saved my life. He knew the signs that something bad was going to happen and he carried me to safety.* "
> —Amber Owen

BHOORI

Ning Nong isn't the only animal to have saved a life. In 2010 a cow named Bhoori rescued a grandmother when sudden floods hit Pakistan. Zainab Bibi, who was 70 years old, was washed away from her home in the heavy rain. She thought she was going to die, until Bhoori appeared next to her in the water. She held tight to her cow's neck while the two of them floated for hours, before reaching the safety of higher ground.

Trees were falling and houses were being swept away, but Ning Nong kept moving, forcing himself through the raging current. He struggled on, step by step, as the wave kept coming until, finally, the exhausted elephant reached a wall. He lowered himself so that Amber could climb off. They were safe!

MAKING HISTORY

Ning Nong's determination had saved Amber's life. People around the world were horrified when they heard about the tsunami, but the story of Ning Nong and Amber gave them some good news too. The children's writer Michael Morpurgo even wrote a book based on their escape, called *Running Wild*. And when Amber got home to England, she decided to send money every year to help the elephants of Thailand have a better life.

It was a kind thing for Amber to do—and an important one too. Elephants are magnificent animals that deserve our care. And thanks to Ning Nong, we also know they can be very alert, very clever, and very, very brave.

Phuket was very badly damaged by the tsunami (*above*), and Michael Morpurgo wrote a book about Ning Nong's rescue called *Running Wild* (*right*).

SERGEANT STUBBY

The stray dog who became a war hero

OUT OF THE ORDINARY

Sometimes we find heroes in very unexpected places. When a stray dog with short legs and droopy eyes wandered onto an American army base in July 1917, no one could have believed that he would become one of the most celebrated military animals of all time. And if one of the soldiers, Corporal Robert Conroy, hadn't seen that the dog needed looking after, maybe this story would be very different. But Robert did notice, and he took care of their little visitor. He named him Stubby because of his small, waggy tail—and the rest, as they say, is history.

Stubby was born in either 1916 or 1917. He was a terrier with a shiny black nose, dark eyes, and a brown-and-white coat. When he was found walking across an army training field in Connecticut, he was just a puppy, with no home to go to. Robert and the other soldiers quickly became attached to Stubby, so when they had to sail across the Atlantic Ocean to Europe to fight in the First World War, Robert decided to smuggle the dog onto the ship.

When the commanding officer noticed the animal on board, he got angry. But the soldiers had taught Stubby how to "salute" by raising one paw, and when the officer saw this, he was so impressed that he let the dog stay. Stubby, still very young, was on his way to France. He was given special tags to hang around his neck, just like the soldiers, and when he arrived in Europe, he showed just how much he deserved to wear them.

OUT AT WAR

Wherever Robert and the other soldiers went, Stubby followed—even onto the battlefield. While loud gunfire boomed in the air, he stayed with the men. But he wasn't just fearless—he was also very useful. Whenever the enemy fired poisonous mustard gas at the soldiers, Stubby was the first to smell it, barking loudly to warn his friends to put their gas masks on. He could also hear when bombs were on their way, and howled to make sure the soldiers noticed. He even helped when men got injured, by finding them on the battlefield and barking to let the other soldiers know where he was. And once, when an enemy spy crept into camp, Stubby noticed and made sure he didn't escape.

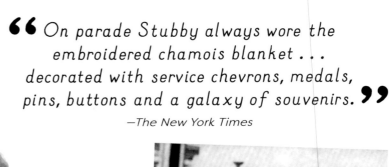

" *On parade Stubby always wore the embroidered chamois blanket . . . decorated with service chevrons, medals, pins, buttons and a galaxy of souvenirs.* **"**
—*The New York Times*

A poster for the animated film based on Stubby's incredible life (*above left*), and Sergeant Stubby wearing his military uniform (*above right*).

By the end of the First World War, Stubby had been in 17 different battles. In one of them he got injured by a grenade and had to be treated by a doctor. The soldiers were so amazed by the dog's courage and determination that he was given lots of medals, which he wore pinned to a special coat. People even started to call him "Sergeant" Stubby, which is a title normally used only for soldiers.

MAKING HISTORY

When he got back to the United States, Stubby's adventures became well known. He went to live with Robert, led a big military parade, and met three different American presidents! When he died in 1926, his body was displayed at the Smithsonian National Museum of American History, where you can still see it today. He had several books written about him, and almost exactly 100 years after his time on the battlefield, he even had an animated film made about his life. Stubby was a faithful dog and an incredible example of how animals can make a real difference to people's lives. He was definitely one of the smallest heroes of the First World War, but it's hard to think of any that displayed quite so much bravery.

" *He led the American troops in a pass and review parade and later visited with President Woodrow Wilson. He visited the White House twice and met Presidents Harding and Coolidge.* **"**
—Smithsonian National Museum of American History

BINTI JUA

The gorilla who rescued a little boy

IN THE ZOO

Some of the most incredible animals on the planet are also some of the most dangerous. Think of lions, great white sharks, or saltwater crocodiles—they're all intelligent, fast, and very powerful, but most people wouldn't want to be trapped anywhere with one! The same is true of gorillas. They're extraordinary animals, and they're often very calm, but they're also far stronger than humans and they can turn violent when they're angry. So, when a three-year-old boy fell into the gorilla enclosure at a zoo, people understandably got very frightened. What was going to happen to him?

The entrance to Brookfield Zoo near Chicago, where Binti Jua lived.

Before we find out, let's meet one of the seven gorillas who lived in the enclosure. Her name was Binti Jua, and although she was just eight years old when the accident happened, she had already grown to a heavy weight. She was a western lowland gorilla with muscular arms, dark hair, and gleaming brown eyes. Her home was Brookfield Zoo, near Chicago.

AN UNEXPECTED VISITOR

It was a warm August day in 1996 when Binti Jua and the other gorillas at the zoo suddenly had a very unexpected visitor. Their enclosure was a big pit with high walls, so that children could look down at them and get a good view. But one three-year-old boy was so excited that he got far closer than he should have. Before grown-ups could stop him, he climbed over the barrier and stood right on top of the wall. Then, disastrously, he slipped into the enclosure.

The boy fell 24 feet, hitting his head so hard that he couldn't get up from the floor. People screamed. The little boy was all alone with the gorillas! Would he be okay? Would the animals harm him? Everyone panicked. The gorillas ran around, unsure what to do—all except Binti Jua, who was actually carrying her own baby on her back. She approached the unmoving boy and gently picked him up, as if he were as light as a doll.

Still, the visitors who were watching were terrified. What was she going to do with him? They soon realized, however, that they had no reason to worry. Binti Jua, with her baby on her back and the boy in her arms, took the boy slowly through the enclosure to a door where the zookeepers could reach them. Then she cradled the boy in her lap and kept him safe, waiting patiently for the keepers to come and help.

> **66** *The nation's hairiest Good Samaritan is reaping the rewards of her good heart today. Lots of visitors and baskets of fruit from adoring fans—all for Binti Jua.* **99**
> —ABC News

MAKING HISTORY

It was an amazing act of care. The little boy made a full recovery, and his rescue appeared in news stories all over the world. Binti Jua—whose name translates, rather beautifully, as "Daughter of Sunshine"—became very well known, and lots of visitors came to the zoo to see her.

So why had she protected an injured child? Some experts thought that because she had been looked after by zookeepers when she was a baby, she had a close connection with humans. Others thought that she was just doing something natural and motherly. Whatever the truth was, Binti Jua gave us even more proof that while some people might think of gorillas as scary, they can also be extremely sensitive.

TRAKR

The dog who found the last survivor after 9/11

A TRAGIC DAY

Police dogs often find themselves in very dangerous situations. They have to be brave, calm, and hardworking, and they need lots of training to get them ready to do their job. They use their eyes and ears to think quickly, their legs to run fast, and their noses to sniff things out. A well-trained police dog is an amazing animal—which is exactly how we can describe Trakr, the hero of this story.

September 11, 2001, was a tragic day in New York City. Airplanes had flown into its two tallest skyscrapers, and the buildings had collapsed with thousands of people still inside. Many of these people lost their lives straightaway, and others were trapped under a huge pile of rubble. If any of them were to be saved, they needed to be reached quickly. As the city went into chaos and panic, the emergency services sprang into action.

"Search and rescue" dogs were used to hunt for survivors in the wreckage.

TO THE RESCUE

Hundreds of local firefighters rushed to the buildings, and as more and more people heard about what had happened, thousands of rescuers from outside New York raced to the city to try and help them find survivors. One of them was a Canadian police officer named James Symington, who got into his car when he saw the story on the news, despite living almost 14 hours' drive away. With him was his German shepherd police dog, Trakr, who was trained in the Czech Republic and came to Canada as a puppy.

James and Trakr drove through the night to reach New York. By the time they got there, almost a full day had passed since the towers had collapsed. Trakr was around seven years old and had done lots of very valuable work in Canada, helping to catch criminals and find stolen property. But now the lively dog had a new and very important task: saving lives by trying to find people stuck in the wreckage.

THE OTHER DOGS OF 9/11

As many as 300 other dogs helped rescue teams in New York after the towers fell, and there were other heroes too. Roselle was a golden retriever who guided her blind owner out of the buildings before they collapsed, while the job of Nikie—another golden retriever—was to comfort rescue workers in the months afterward.

Trakr with his handler, James, after the amazing rescue.

It was extremely difficult work. The piles of rubble were enormous, and the air was still thick with smoke and dust. But Trakr never gave up. He looked everywhere he could, using his excellent sense of smell to try and find survivors. Was there anyone still alive? As the hours went by, it seemed as though the rescue teams had found everyone they could. But then, a full 27 hours after the buildings had fallen, clever Trakr found what he had been looking for—someone caught in the wreckage, still breathing!

MAKING HISTORY

The person that Trakr had discovered was a woman named Genelle, and she was the last survivor to be found. It was a story that brought people some happiness after such an upsetting event. Today we remember Trakr as an incredible example of an animal who was full of courage and determination—and who showed us the importance of never giving up hope.

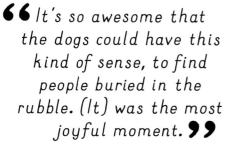

> **"** It's so awesome that the dogs could have this kind of sense, to find people buried in the rubble. (It) was the most joyful moment. **"**
> —Genelle Guzman-McMillan, the woman found by Trakr

He died many years later in 2009, but because he was so special, scientists decided to use a tiny part of his body tissue to create clones, or copies, of the dog. And by the end of the same year, five "mini-Trakr" puppies were born: Trustt, Valor, Solace, Prodigy, and Deja Vu. So even though Trakr may be gone, he will never be forgotten.

DUFFY

The donkey who carried wounded soldiers

DISASTER ON THE BATTLEFIELD

In the sunny Australian city of Adelaide there stands a bronze sculpture of two men and a very tired-looking donkey. One of the men is guiding the donkey, the other is sitting on its back. The animal in the statue never once set foot in Australia but has become a well-known part of that country's history. And the reason why? Because of something that happened more than 100 years ago, on the other side of the world.

The First World War was a very scary time. Fierce battles were being fought in lots of different countries. For the soldiers of Australia and New Zealand, however, one battle is remembered more than any other: the Gallipoli Campaign, which took place in what is now Turkey. It was a time when troops from Australia, New Zealand, Britain, Ireland, and France were trying to capture an important area of land from the enemy. Except not everything went to plan.

A statue to remember Duffy and the people he helped in the war.

On April 25, 1915, thousands of Australian and New Zealand soldiers received orders to sail into a small bay and land on shore. They were hoping to catch the enemy, but this was much harder than they thought. The soldiers who made it to land found themselves stuck near the coast and under fire. Over the next days and weeks, many of them were killed or badly wounded. And at this very difficult time, a donkey became an unlikely hero.

DONKEY WORK

No one knows for sure how or why the young soldier John Simpson Kirkpatrick managed to find a donkey near the fighting. Maybe the animal had been carrying water for the troops. Maybe it came from a local farmer. John was a stretcher-bearer—someone who carried injured men to safety—but as the bullets flew and the soldiers at Gallipoli began falling, he soon realized he needed more than a stretcher. This is how the donkey found itself in the middle of a very frightening battle.

John began picking up the wounded men and placing them on the donkey, using the animal to lead them down the rocky valley and back to the safety of the beach. The noise of the fighting would have been horrible, but day after day, week after week, the hardworking donkey carried badly injured soldiers down a hilly path and away from the danger.

> 66 *Private Simpson and his little beast earned the admiration of everyone ... They worked all day and night.* 99
>
> —Colonel John Monash, who also fought in the battle

Duffy and John helping a soldier with a wounded leg.

Stories can sometimes get confused during wartime. Some say the donkey was named Abdul, or Murphy, but the name that most often gets spoken about is Duffy. Some people even say that John used more than one donkey to rescue his fellow soldiers. We can say for certain, however, that over 24 long days many men's lives were saved by making a risky journey on the back of a calm and sure-footed donkey.

MAKING HISTORY

The story has become famous. Legend has it that as many as 300 men were carried down through the valley by Duffy and John. Every year, on April 25, the people of Australia and New Zealand have a special day called Anzac Day to remember the landings at Gallipoli, and the lives that were lost. They remember the men who fought and died there. They remember the soldiers who survived and battled to the end. And they remember one man and a very brave, important donkey, without whom many more lives would have been lost.

LIN WANG

WARTIME WORK

Not many animals have served in two different armies and lived long enough to have 86 birthdays. In fact, there's almost certainly only ever been one. Lin Wang was a unique elephant who led an amazing life. He saw and did things that most elephants never do, living to an incredible age and becoming one of the most famous animals in Asia.

He was born in 1917, in a hot Southeast Asian country called Myanmar, known as Burma at the time. We don't know very much about his early years, but like all young elephants, he would have quickly grown big and powerful. In those days, some armies still used elephants during wartime, because the animals were strong enough to pull very heavy things. So when Japanese soldiers invaded Myanmar in the Second World War, they started using local elephants to lift their equipment. One of them was Lin Wang.

Carrying things around for an army isn't something an elephant would ever choose to do, and it was probably very hard work. For the soldiers, however, it was very useful. So useful, in fact, that Lin Wang would soon be part of another army. In 1943, a big group of Chinese soldiers arrived in Myanmar to fight the Japanese. When they saw Lin Wang, they captured him, along with 12 other elephants.

He now found himself hauling logs and heavy weapons for the Chinese army. The new soldiers were very impressed by Lin Wang, who was only 26 years old but was already a very fine-looking elephant with shining white tusks. They started calling him Ah Mei, which means "the Beautiful."

GROWING OLD

But Lin Wang's journey was just beginning. Soon he and the other elephants had to march north to China. Lin Wang was taken to the island of Taiwan, where at first he had to do more lifting work. Then, in 1954, the army decided that it would be better if he lived in a zoo.

Lin Wang with a Chinese soldier during the war.

It was here in Taipei Zoo that a keeper gave him the name that we now use: Lin Wang, meaning "King of the Forest." He spent the rest of his life in the zoo—and what a long life it was! Many elephants never live past their sixtieth birthday, but Lin Wang grew older and older, becoming more and more famous. People gave him the nickname "Grandpa Lin" because he was getting so old. The zoo even had a special celebration for his sixty-sixth birthday, with so many people coming to see him that the zoo began holding birthday celebrations for "Grandpa Lin" every year.

> **"Lin Wang symbolizes the common memories of four generations of people.... We watched him grow old, and he was ever-present when we grew up."**
> —Ma Ying-jeou, the mayor of Taipei

> **'Grandpa Lin was more than just an impressively old elephant—he was a cultural icon, a creature whose legacy is woven into several countries' histories.'**
> —ABC News

MAKING HISTORY

Lin Wang lived until he was 86 years old, becoming the oldest known Asian elephant the world had ever seen. He was even included in *Guinness World Records*. The elderly elephant was so popular that when he died in 2003, thousands of people came to say their goodbyes. Children were given free entry to the zoo to come and remember him, and the local mayor made Lin Wang an "honorary citizen of Taipei," which meant he would never be forgotten by the people of the city.

Lin Wang's body has been preserved and is still on display at Taipei Zoo. It's a way of reminding the world that Lin Wang was a unique elephant with a very unique story.

LAIKA
The space dog

STRAY IN SPACE

This is the story of a small dog who changed history. She was brown and white with pointy ears, and she lived alone on the streets of Moscow, in Russia. She had no family and no home. Most people never even noticed her. Then one day she was collected by scientists who worked at a space center. They named her Laika—which in Russian means "barker"—and soon the whole world would know her name.

In the 1950s, there was a lot of competition between Russia (or the Soviet Union, as it was called then) and the United States. They were both trying to become the first country to send humans into space. The Russians had built some very powerful spacecraft, but they didn't know if they would be safe for human astronauts. So to check if it was possible to stay alive in a spacecraft, they decided to put a dog inside and send it into space. Laika didn't understand it, but this would be her mission.

> **"** *Laika was quiet and charming. I wanted to do something nice for her.* **"**
> —Dr. Vladimir Yazdovsky, the scientist who took Laika home to meet his children

LAUNCHED INTO ORBIT

The Russian scientists began by training her. They kept her in a small kennel, a bit like the spacecraft cockpit, so that she could get used to having very little room to move. To prepare her for the feeling of being in space, they put her in a centrifuge—a big machine that spins around and around. They also gave her special food that was a bit like jelly, which was what she would need to eat in the spacecraft. The scientists at the space center liked Laika very much—one of them even took her home to play with his children. But her big day was getting nearer.

Laika trained for the mission in specially designed space equipment.

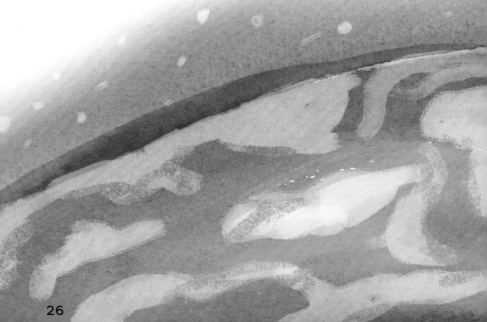

On November 3, 1957, a spacecraft called *Sputnik 2* blasted off from the Russian countryside and shot into the sky. It was a silver-colored cone about 13 feet high. The spacecraft was full of radio transmitters and other machines, so the people in the space center could find out what was happening on board. It also had a passenger. The dog who had grown up on the lonely streets of Moscow was now the first-ever living creature in space. She was probably only two years old, but Laika had become the world's first astronaut.

MAKING HISTORY

We don't know exactly how long she lived on her extraordinary mission high above Earth. But what we do know is that, although she was alive for several hours after takeoff, she didn't survive the whole journey. When the news about Laika reached the rest of the world, some people were angry that the Russians had used a dog in this way. Other people thought that because of Laika, we had discovered much more about space travel.

No one had asked Laika if she wanted to be an astronaut, and her experience would have been very scary. But her voyage in *Sputnik 2* was now world-famous. Laika appeared on badges, stamps, cards, and posters. In Moscow, more than 50 years after her journey, they even put up a special statue to thank her. Now we can say that without the first dog in space, there would have been no first human in space. Laika was gentle and trusting, and her life helped us to understand that space travel was possible. For that, she is remembered as one of the greatest animals that ever lived.

Laika appeared on a Polish postage stamp, alongside *Sputnik 2*.

> **"** *The Soviet Union has launched the first ever living creature into the cosmos . . . traveling nearly 1,500 kilometers above the Earth.* **"**
> —BBC news report, November 1957

LOBO

WOLF IN THE WILD

Wolves would not make good pets. They are wild, cunning, and strong, with dagger-sharp teeth and thick fur. They prowl, they growl, and they howl in the dead of night. People have always been afraid of wolves, but they can be impressive animals. No wolf is a better example than Lobo, who lived in the wilderness of New Mexico. He was very big and very fierce. They called him the King of Currumpaw.

In those days, people tried to hunt wolves to stop them attacking their cows and sheep. And in the rocky Currumpaw Valley, where Lobo lived, there were lots of wolves to hunt. It was October 1893 when a man named Ernest Thompson Seton arrived in the area with his gun. He already knew about Lobo because people had told him about a large gray wolf who had eaten hundreds of cattle. Many hunters had tried and failed to trap him. Ernest was an expert at hunting wolves and he wanted to be the one to catch Lobo.

Ernest Thompson Seton was an expert hunter and later became a successful writer, artist, and naturalist.

But it wasn't going to be easy. Lobo wasn't just enormous. He was also very smart. He was the leader of a pack of five other wolves, who had been killing cows and sheep for years. Whenever humans appeared, the wolves vanished into the hills. The local cowboys and shepherds offered a thousand-dollar reward for anyone who could stop Lobo and his pack. Ernest needed a plan.

TERRIBLE TRAPS

He decided to leave four big lumps of poisoned meat in the places where Lobo hunted. The next day he went to see if they had been taken. The first lump had disappeared. So had the second, and the third. Ernest was very pleased—he thought Lobo must have eaten them. But when he reached the fourth lump, he had a surprise: Lobo had simply carried the other three lumps there and left them all in a pile, uneaten.

None of Ernest's ideas seemed to work. He set traps, but Lobo avoided them. He tried more poison, but Lobo always smelled it and stayed away. The wolf was too clever to be caught. Eventually, Ernest came up with a new plan. He noticed that Lobo was very fond of a white female in the pack named Blanca, so he captured her instead. Ernest hoped that when he took her away, Lobo would follow him. It was another trap.

When Lobo realized that Blanca was gone, he howled sadly for days. Then he tried to find her by following her smell. This was a terrible mistake for Lobo. Ernest had set more than 100 traps around the area, and the next morning he found Lobo lying helpless, with all four of his legs stuck. Finally, Ernest had caught the wolf. But when he raised his gun to shoot, something stopped him. He looked at Lobo—the mighty wolf who had shown so much bravery, love, and intelligence—and he lowered his gun. Killing him like this was impossible. But Lobo's fight was soon over—he died less than a day later from the injuries he'd gotten from the traps.

> ❛ Ever since Lobo, my sincerest wish has been to impress upon people that each of our native wild creatures is in itself a precious heritage. ❜❜
>
> —Ernest Thompson Seton

MAKING HISTORY

His experiences with Lobo had a very big effect on Ernest. When he wrote a book about wild animals, the first story was about Lobo. It helped people to see wolves very differently. And that wasn't all. Ernest also changed the way that America looked after its wild places. He worked to make sure that wolves and other animals had enough space to live in. He even helped to start the Boy Scouts of America and other important projects that taught children about nature and the outdoors. And he never, ever forgot the fearless gray wolf who once ruled the hills: Lobo, the King of Currumpaw.

Lobo inspired Ernest to help start the Boy Scouts of America, which teaches children the importance of nature and the outdoors.

ZARAFA

OUT OF AFRICA

Many animals make great journeys, but very few have ever traveled as far as Zarafa. The beautiful giraffe began her life on the plains of Africa and ended it among the grand boulevards of Paris, after walking almost the full length of France.

Her story began in 1824, when the viceroy of Egypt—a powerful ruler—decided to send a gift to the king of France. In those days, it was common for royals and leaders to exchange luxurious presents, as a way of showing their wealth and friendship. But rather than sending expensive jewels or silks, the viceroy chose something more unusual. He wanted to give the king a giraffe.

Zarafa was just a baby when she was captured by hunters in the African wilderness. She was too weak to walk properly, so she had to be strapped to a camel and carried to the banks of the Nile River.

From there, she was taken down the river on a small boat to the Mediterranean Sea, where a sailing ship was waiting for her. The ceilings on board were too low for Zarafa, so a hole was cut in the deck so she could poke her head and neck into the open air. The ship carried her more than 1,550 miles across the waves to Europe and the French city of Marseille.

This would have been an enormous shock for a young giraffe. It was an enormous shock for the people of Marseille, too. No giraffe had ever set foot in France before, so the arrival of Zarafa, with her long neck, elegant eyelashes, and spotted coat, caused a sensation. Her epic journey, however, was just beginning. The king lived in Paris, 500 miles to the north. There was no easy way to transport a giraffe across the land, so it was decided that Zarafa would have to walk.

PROGRESS TO PARIS

Her incredible march through France began in May 1827. Helping to look after her was a naturalist—an expert who knew a lot about animals. He made sure she was wearing a special yellow cloak to keep her warm and shoes to protect her feet. She was also joined on her journey by a small herd of cows, who provided the milk Zarafa needed to stay strong. She was still a young giraffe, but she was growing fast.

> **66** *The giraffe occupies all the public's attention; one talks of nothing else in the circles of the capital.* **99**
> —*La Pandore* newspaper

There was excitement in Paris as thousands of people came to see a giraffe for the first time.

In every town she passed through, people rushed to catch a glimpse of this tall, exotic creature from a distant land. When she reached the city of Lyon, 30,000 people crowded the streets to see her. Zarafa was becoming a celebrity. She trod on, day after day, week after week. She passed orchards and vineyards, hills and forests, castles and villages. Finally, more than 40 days after leaving Marseille, and 3,000 miles away from the plains of Africa where she had been born, the giraffe arrived in Paris.

MAKING HISTORY

The people of the city were amazed by Zarafa. She was presented to the king at his palace, then taken to her new home in a famous garden: the Jardin des Plantes. More than 100,000 Parisians came to admire her. Artists came to paint her picture, writers wrote stories about her, and bakers made special giraffe cookies in her honor. Some ladies even wore spotted dresses and had their hair arranged in towering, giraffe-like hairstyles!

Zarafa remained in Paris all her life. She stayed in the Jardin des Plantes for the next 18 years, dying peacefully in 1845. Today her body is still displayed in a museum in the French city of La Rochelle—a tribute to a remarkable, and very brave, giraffe.

Cookies shaped like Zarafa were popular in the bakeries of Paris.

MONTAUCIEL

The sheep who was a passenger in the first hot-air balloon

INCREDIBLE INVENTIONS

Sheep are lovable animals, but they don't often surprise us. When we spot them in the countryside, they're usually grazing in fields or resting in barns. Perhaps—because sheep are very good climbers—we might even notice them high up mountains. But have you ever seen a sheep riding in a hot-air balloon? For that extraordinary sight, we need to travel way back to France in the 1780s.

It was a time before airplanes and helicopters, a time when the only things that could be seen in the sky were birds and clouds. But in a French town called Annonay, there were two grown-up brothers who wanted to change that. Their names were Joseph-Michel and Jacques-Étienne Montgolfier. They had 14 other brothers and sisters, but as well as having a very big family, they had a very big idea, too.

The Montgolfier brothers, Joseph-Michel and Jacques-Étienne, inventors of the hot-air balloon.

The brothers hoped to invent something that had never been seen before: a balloon that would carry passengers into the air. They noticed that paper bags placed over a fire would float upward because of the hot air trapped inside the bag. They wanted to see if something bigger would float in the same way. It was going to be a completely new kind of transport—and it would carry one sheep into the history books.

To try out their idea, they made a very large balloon from paper and cloth, leaving a hole at the bottom where the hot air could get in. On June 4, 1783, they took it to the town marketplace and burned a pile of straw and wool underneath. Sure enough, the balloon filled with hot air from the fire and started to float up into the sky! The people watching were very impressed. But the balloon wasn't carrying any passengers—and this was the brothers' next plan.

UP, UP, AND AWAY

Three months later, on September 19, they were ready to show their balloon invention to the king of France, Louis XVI, and his wife, Marie Antoinette, at the Palace of Versailles near Paris. This time, it wouldn't just be a hot-air balloon—it would be a hot-air balloon with passengers. A huge crowd had come to watch: some say more than 100,000 people!

Because the brothers weren't sure if humans would be able to ride in the balloon's basket, they had chosen three animal passengers instead: a duck, a rooster, and a sheep. It was the first time something like this had ever been tried, so the brothers were using the animals to check that it was safe. The animals didn't understand it, of course, but they were about to make history.

> " To general amazement, the balloon rose 500 meters above the crowd, coming down eight minutes later to cheers ... The aeronaut sheep, called Montauciel, ended its days peacefully in the sheepfold of the queen. "
> —*Le Figaro* newspaper

As the enormous crowd looked on, the balloon and its passengers rose around 1,600 feet above the palace. The animals stayed in the air for eight whole minutes and landed about two miles away. Most importantly, they had all survived. When people reached them, they found the sheep happily nibbling on the grass. It had no idea that it had just become one of the first hot-air-balloon passengers in the world, but it was named Montauciel, which means "climb to the sky" in French.

MAKING HISTORY

We don't know what happened to the brave duck and rooster, but we know that Montauciel was taken to live in the royal zoo for the rest of its life, white-fleeced and well-fed. Hundreds of years later, we remember Montauciel and its two feathered friends for helping us to understand that balloon flights with passengers were possible. So the next time you see a sheep in a field or a hot-air balloon in the sky, give a thought to the woolly animal that once floated high above France.

HUBERTA

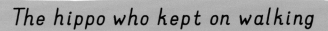

The hippo who kept on walking

ON THE MOVE

South Africa is famous around the world for its wildlife. It has fearsome lions, tall giraffes, and brightly feathered birds. It has rhinos and elephants, leopards and cheetahs, crocodiles and hippos. And what wonderful creatures hippos are! They wallow in mud, honk loudly, and eat enough grass and plants to stay looking big and fat. But in 1928, one bold hippo did something much more unusual. Her name was Huberta, and she went for a walk that lasted two and a half years.

Huberta crossed the Tugela River in KwaZulu-Natal, and walked on toward Port Elizabeth.

Huberta was born in a part of the country called KwaZulu-Natal, close to a wide river where lots of hippos still live today. No one really knows why she started walking south one day. Some people think she was looking for a friend that she'd lost. Other people think she was trying to get as far away from the river as possible, maybe because her mother had died there. Some even think she was trying to return to a place where other hippos used to live long ago. But whatever made her start wandering, her journey would be an unforgettable one.

EAST LONDON

ADVENTURE THROUGH AFRICA

Soon after leaving the river in late 1928, she caught people's attention. It was very strange to see a hippo on its own, walking across roads and fields. In November a photographer took her picture as she was walking through some farmland. When it appeared in the newspaper, people became very interested in her journey. At first the newspapers called her Hubert, because they thought she was male, but when they realized she was female, they changed her name to Huberta. And as she moved farther and farther south, more and more people heard about her adventure.

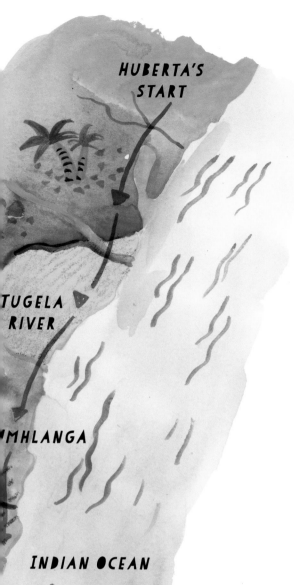

HUBERTA'S START

TUGELA RIVER

MHLANGA

INDIAN OCEAN

She walked and she walked and she walked. For months she plodded through towns and villages, over railway lines, and across gardens—often stopping to chomp the grass! She waddled over golf courses and along beaches. She rested for a long while at a town called Umhlanga, where crowds of people came to see her, and then she kept going. One evening she even fell asleep on a railway track, and a train driver had to wake her up and move her out of the way!

Huberta was now traveling through places where no hippo had lived for a very long time, but this didn't mean she was easy to spot. She usually walked at night, so often people would only see her big footprints the next day. And when hunters tried to catch her and put her in a zoo, they found it impossible. Huberta didn't want to be stopped.

> **"** *Huberta wandered away from Zululand in 1928 . . . through ports and settled communities where hippos had long been unknown.* **"**
> —Hedley A. Chilvers, the author of *Huberta Goes South*

MAKING HISTORY

By now, she was famous right across South Africa. In March 1931, around 30 months after beginning her walk, she arrived close to a seaside city called East London. She had crossed more than 100 rivers, and was now almost six hundred miles from where she had started. But Huberta's journey was about to end. One day, she was found dead in the water. It was very sad news, and when her body was stuffed and put on show in a museum, more than 20,000 people came to visit her in just five weeks.

Today her body can be seen in Amathole Museum near East London, South Africa. And although we'll never know exactly why she made her epic walk, we know Huberta was a hippo who never gave up—and who definitely wasn't afraid to follow her own path.

BALTO

The husky who helped save the lives of children

A DIFFICULT WINTER

Balto was a black-and-white husky who was born in 1919. He has a very special place in American history, because of the remarkable journey he and his fellow huskies made one winter.

The state of Alaska is a fierce place over the coldest months—a vast land of ice, snow, and freezing temperatures. For many animals, it would be impossible to survive. But for huskies, a very tough, loyal breed of dog, this weather is exactly what they're used to. So in 1925, when a remote Alaskan town had an emergency, it was huskies who came to the rescue.

Did you know?

Balto was named after Samuel J. Balto, who, along with Fridtjof Nansen, first crossed the Greenland Ice Cap in 1888.

The winter of 1925 was horribly cold—it reached minus 49°F!—and in the coastal town of Nome, children began to fall ill. The doctors quickly realized it was a nasty infection called diphtheria. In those days, diphtheria was very contagious, which means it could spread easily from one person to another. It was also very, very dangerous—the children would die if they didn't get the right injections. The doctors needed the right antitoxin, or medicine, as quickly as possible.

But there was a big problem. The only antitoxin was more than 746 miles away in the city of Anchorage, across endless icy plains. No trucks could handle the rough, snowy ground, there were no boats, and the weather was far too cold for the only airplane—its engine was completely frozen. There was only one option: to put the antitoxin on a train to the nearest station, then use teams of huskies to carry it the last 674 miles to Nome. It was a very risky plan, and might take too long to reach the children, but they had to try.

> **"** Some consider (it) the finest feat in dog-and-human history, a 1925 race to deliver lifesaving diphtheria serum to icebound Nome, Alaska. **"**
> — The New York Times

HUSKIES TO THE RESCUE

They started immediately. The first part of the journey went well, and the antitoxin reached the station. Then the dogs took over. Nome was much too far away to be reached by one team of huskies, so they had to use a relay of different dog teams, with one team running until it reached the next. Each team pulled the sled of a driver, called a musher, who carried the antitoxin. And gradually, the medicine got nearer and nearer to Nome.

The husky teams ran and ran through the freezing wilderness, speeding into the wind. The first team covered 50 miles, the next 30. On they ran through day and night, team by team, as blinding blizzards roared all around them. One team got its lines tangled when they nearly hit a reindeer. Another team had to cross the ice of a frozen bay. But nothing stopped them. And with 50 miles left to go, it was the turn of Balto's team.

Balto ran like a wild thing, leading his team and his musher through the dark, snowy night as though he understood it was a matter of life and death. But when they got to the last team— disaster!—the musher was fast asleep, and his dogs weren't ready. Balto and his team couldn't wait. They charged on, exhausted from their efforts but still running hard, until finally, more than five days after the first dogs had started the journey, they arrived in Nome. Thanks to the heart, speed, and amazing stamina of the huskies, the children now had their medicine. They were saved.

> **"** Children and others frequently climb up on (Balto's statue) for a photo op, or to contemplate life and the stirring words on the statue's plaque: Endurance, Fidelity, Intelligence. **"**
> —the website of Central Park, New York

MAKING HISTORY

Balto became famous because he was the lead dog of the team that reached Nome. He soon had his own statue in Central Park, in New York, and appeared on the front page of all the newspapers. But he was just one of 150 huskies who helped save the children's lives, and every single dog ran bravely. It takes a lot of determination to keep running through howling storms and winter gales—and it's this determination that turned the huskies of Alaska into heroes.

The bronze statue of Balto in New York City's Central Park, which children love to climb.

EMILY

The cow who made a great escape

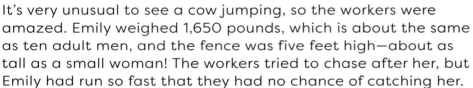

A SCARY START

Not all animals live free. Some get taken to places that are very scary for them, where they can't run around and don't come out alive. These places are called slaughterhouses, or abattoirs. In 1995 in Massachusetts, one cow was taken to a place like this and decided she didn't like it at all. She didn't want to be turned into meat—so she did something about it. This is the story of Emily, a young cow who made a brave leap for freedom.

It was a cold November's day, and the people who worked at the slaughterhouse were taking a break. Suddenly, something happened that they'd never seen before. One of the cows that was about to be killed took a run-up at the slaughterhouse fence, jumped right over the top, and disappeared into the snowy countryside! This was Emily, a three-year-old cow whose daring escape was about to make her a star.

It's very unusual to see a cow jumping, so the workers were amazed. Emily weighed 1,650 pounds, which is about the same as ten adult men, and the fence was five feet high—about as tall as a small woman! The workers tried to chase after her, but Emily had run so fast that they had no chance of catching her.

ON THE RUN

They came up with a plan to trap her, by leaving piles of fresh hay on the ground. They thought Emily would come and eat the hay, but she was too smart for that. She stayed away from the slaughterhouse, and as the days went on, the workers still couldn't catch her. Luckily for Emily, she had enough to eat because some of the people who lived nearby helped her by leaving out food in their backyards. And she seemed to be enjoying her adventure— she was even seen running through the woods with a herd of deer!

When the newspapers heard about the cow's escape, her story appeared all around the world. But one local family wanted to do more than just read about Emily: they wanted to look after her. Lewis and Meg Randa and their three children lived close by in a place called the Peace Abbey. They were vegetarians, which means they didn't eat meat, and they thought it was very important that Emily stayed safe.

CINCINNATI FREEDOM

Seven years after Emily made her escape, another cow did exactly the same thing! This time, it happened near the city of Cincinnati in Ohio, and the cow spent 11 days running free before she was caught and taken to live in an animal sanctuary. And the name she was given? Cincinnati Freedom!

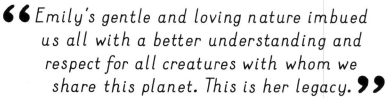

> 66 Emily's gentle and loving nature imbued us all with a better understanding and respect for all creatures with whom we share this planet. This is her legacy. 99
>
> —the Peace Abbey

Because no one had been able to catch the runaway cow, the slaughterhouse agreed to sell Emily to Lewis and Meg for just one dollar. And six weeks after her escape—on December 24, 1995—the family managed to find Emily, gently coax her on to a trailer, and bring her to the Peace Abbey gardens to live with them.

Meg and Lewis with their children and Emily enjoying her new home.

MAKING HISTORY

Over the next seven and a half years, this is where Emily spent her time. For the thousands of people who came to visit her, she became a symbol of hope and survival, and when she died a natural death in 2003, she was buried in the gardens behind a statue of the famous Indian leader Mahatma Gandhi. Like Gandhi, Emily wanted a peaceful life and had the courage to try and change things. Today there's a life-size bronze statue of Emily at the Peace Abbey, wrapped in a blanket and decorated with flowers, remembering a very daring—and very special—cow.

WILLIAM WINDSOR

AN ARMY TRADITION

Goats usually keep to themselves. Most of them are quiet, patient, and rather serious-looking, whether they're clambering up mountains or grazing in fields. But when one very handsome goat ended up becoming a famous member of the British Army, it showed us that they could also be very lively characters. His name was William Windsor—or Billy for short—and he was no ordinary billy goat.

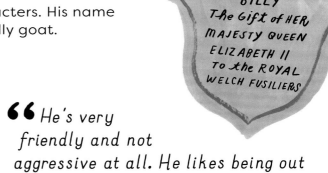

BILLY
The Gift of HER MAJESTY QUEEN ELIZABETH II to the ROYAL WELCH FUSILIERS

> **He's very friendly and not aggressive at all. He likes being out and about and meeting people.**
> —Captain Nick Zorab, British Army

It might sound strange, but there have actually been goats in the British Army for hundreds of years. People say that the tradition started in 1775, when a wild goat walked onto a battlefield where a regiment—or special group—of British soldiers were fighting. The goat helped to lead the soldiers off the field, so the same regiment has had a goat as a mascot ever since. In 1884 Queen Victoria even presented the regiment with a goat from her royal herd. When animals are given to the army by a king or queen, they aren't just mascots—they get treated as real soldiers!

And the tradition has continued. Billy, a Kashmir goat with a long white coat and magnificent curved horns, was born in the year 2000, and he was presented to the regiment just a year later, as a gift from the queen. Suddenly the army regiment had a new member to join its men—one special goat!

PARADES AND PROMOTION

One of Billy's main jobs was to stay calm at all times, especially during noisy parades and big events, and he was very good at this. He was so well behaved, in fact, that he got a promotion, which means he was made even more important. Billy the goat was now Lance Corporal William Windsor—and junior soldiers had to stand to attention and salute him! He even had his own handler to take care of him: a soldier named Dai, who was known as the goat major.

Like all goats, Billy enjoyed eating. Sometimes he ate things that most goats never get to try. As well as his normal food, Dai was allowed to give him two cigarettes a day to eat, and from time to time he even had beer to drink.

But Billy wasn't always perfect. In 2006, five years after he joined the army, he was leading a big parade to celebrate the queen's birthday when he started walking so fast that Dai couldn't control him. Not only that, but he tried to headbutt one of the army drummers! Poor Billy was demoted for his bad behavior, which means he had his lance corporal title taken away.

William at the 90th anniversary celebration of the Royal British Legion.

However, Billy was a very good-natured goat, and just three months later his commanding officer was so pleased with him that he was made a lance corporal again. And that's how he stayed for another three years, walking at the head of grand parades and being saluted by soldiers.

> 66 *Billy performed exceptionally well. He has had all summer to reflect on his behavior at the queen's birthday and clearly earned the rank he deserves.* 99
> —Captain Nick Zorab

MAKING HISTORY

In 2009, after eight years of loyal service at home and overseas, he was retired from the army and went to live in a wildlife park near London. The regiment has a new goat now, but Dai and the other soldiers have never forgotten Billy, the four-legged lance corporal who was usually peaceful, often hungry—and sometimes full of mischief!

William with his handler, Lance Corporal Dai Davies.

41

CLARA

The rhino who toured Europe

BEGINNINGS IN INDIA

Rhinos are many things. They are strong, solid, huge, and thick-skinned—and much more besides! But you probably wouldn't ever think to describe a rhino as "well-traveled." This, however, is the best way to sum up one unforgettable Indian rhinoceros who lived in the 18th century. Her name was Clara, and over the course of her life she saw more of Europe than most people ever do.

Her story begins in 1738 in India, where she was a wobbly-legged calf living in the wild. Clara was left all alone at only a few months old when her mother was shot by hunters. A Dutchman who was living nearby found the orphaned rhino and decided to take her home and look after her. His new horned houseguest was allowed to come indoors, meet visitors, and sometimes even eat from the table!

Clara attracted lots of attention, and soon she was sold to another local Dutchman named Mr. Van der Meer. It was a time when not many people around the world had ever seen a real-life rhino, and Mr. Van der Meer realized that people back in Europe might even pay to see an unusual creature like Clara. His moneymaking idea meant that Clara was about to start a journey that would last around 17 years.

> ❝ It's difficult to imagine the impact that a female Indian rhinoceros could have had on 18th-century Europe . . . (she was) the equivalent of a modern-day rock star. ❞
>
> —J. Paul Getty Trust

FAR FROM HOME

The first thing he had to do was transport a fast-growing rhinoceros over the sea from India to the Netherlands. The journey took them months. Clara was kept in a cage on deck, and while the long trip would certainly have been tough for her, the sailors gave her rubdowns with fish oil to make sure her skin didn't get too dry.

They also fed her regularly and found she had a special liking for oranges! Finally, in July 1741, she was led off the ship and into the port city of Leiden. People could barely believe their eyes. Europe now had its very own rhinoceros.

But for Clara and Mr. Van der Meer, this was just the start of their wanderings. The man soon had a special horse-drawn wagon built to carry the rhino from town to town, where he sold tickets to people who wanted to admire her. Clara was quite unlike any creature that Europeans had ever seen—some people even used to think that rhinos were made-up animals!—so she caused flurries of excitement wherever she went.

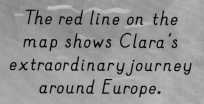

The red line on the map shows Clara's extraordinary journey around Europe.

A painting of Clara by Jean-Baptiste Oudry, 1749.

MAKING HISTORY

And Clara certainly went to lots of places. Over the next 17 years, she traveled to almost every major city in central Europe, chomping huge amounts of hay, bread, and oranges as she grew bigger and bigger. She was visited by royalty in Berlin and Vienna, sailed on a barge up the Rhine River, drew crowds in Switzerland, met the Holy Roman Emperor, impressed the king of France, and became one of the stars of the Venice Carnival. She was examined by scientists, painted by artists, and written about by poets. Some of Europe's most fashionable ladies were so amazed at the sight of Clara that they even started wearing hats that looked like rhino horns!

Clara's grand tour came to an end in London, where she eventually died in 1758. It's difficult to know how many people came to see Clara during her lifetime, but we do know that many of them remarked on how calm and peaceful she was. These days, we understand a lot about rhinos, but hundreds of years ago the European public had to rely on one single animal to learn how incredible a rhino was—and that's why Clara's story is so special.

JUMBO

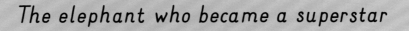

AN AFRICAN ELEPHANT

Elephants are incredible creatures with thick legs, long, curling trunks, and great big barrel-like bodies. Whether they're wandering over the plains, trumpeting through the jungle, or tearing off tree branches for breakfast, these enormous beasts have fascinated humans for thousands of years. So it's no surprise that in the 19th century, people who had only ever seen them in pictures got excited at the thought of seeing one in real life.

For the elephant in this story, things started out as normal. He was born in the bushland of East Africa and did the usual things that baby elephants do: he fed, he learned to walk, and he explored his surroundings. The rest of his life, however, was anything but normal. In 1861, when he was still very young, he was captured by hunters and transported up the Nile River to Cairo in Egypt. From there, he was taken all the way to Paris.

This would have been bewildering and very difficult for any young animal. He now found himself in a zoo in the middle of a busy French city, but before long he was moved again—this time across the sea to London Zoo. Here, the fast-growing elephant was given an African-sounding name by one of the keepers: Jumbo. But this keeper wouldn't have had any idea just how famous the animal—or the name—would become.

Jumbo became famous for giving rides to Victorian visitors (*above*), and elephant toys like this became popular (*left*).

JOINING THE CIRCUS

Jumbo spent nearly 17 years in London, getting bigger and bigger all the time. He was now huge—far taller and heavier than most elephants—and his gentle nature and gigantic size made him incredibly popular with visitors. It's been estimated that during his time at the zoo, he gave rides to more than a million children. So when it was announced that a famous American showman named P. T. Barnum wanted to buy the elephant for his circus, it was reported that 100,000 schoolchildren wrote letters to Queen Victoria to try and stop it happening!

The letters didn't help. In 1882 Jumbo was sold to Barnum's circus and taken across the Atlantic to New York, where huge crowds were waiting to welcome the colossal animal. The elephant immediately became the star attraction in America's most famous circus. People flocked to see him. Songs were sung about him in the music halls, stories were written about him in the newspapers, and souvenirs were sold on the streets.

> 66 *Jumbo the elephant was the most famous animal in the world, and millions of words were written about him in the British and American press.* 99
> —from the book *Jumbo* by W. P. Jolly

Jumbo was the star of P. T. Barnum's "Greatest Show on Earth," which attracted the largest crowds in the history of the circus.

Jumbo had grown to around 11 feet tall, about twice the height of an adult man. And his size meant he was often very hungry. According to an American magazine, Jumbo now ate the following every day: two bales of hay, three bags of onions, two baskets of biscuits, two baskets of oats, and three loaves of bread—as well as apples, oranges, figs, nuts, cakes, sweets, five buckets of water, and a bottle of whiskey!

MAKING HISTORY

Jumbo spent the final three years of his life working in the circus. Mr. Barnum claimed he was the world's biggest elephant. What we can say for certain is that he was one of the world's best known animals. But his life was very unnatural for an elephant, and in many ways would have been extremely hard. Today the word "jumbo" has entered the English language to mean anything huge or enormous. The next time you hear it, make sure you remember the remarkable elephant whose name it was.

LONESOME GEORGE

AN AMAZING DISCOVERY

Giant tortoises don't do things in a hurry. They move through life slowly. They plod, they eat, then they plod some more. It not easy for them to rush away and hide, which is why peop were very surprised in 1971, when a scientist spotted a giant tortoise living on the island of Pinta in the Galápagos Island No one had seen a giant tortoise on Pinta for half a century.

The scientists worked out that the tortoise was a male and around 60 years old. He weighed nearly 165 pounds, which i the same as an adult man, and had been living a quiet life on the island without anyone knowing. It was also discovere that he was the very last giant tortoise of his kind.

Pinta Island tortoises had existed here all through history—but now there was only one left. He was moved to a new home on a nearby island so that he could be looked after, and he was given the name Lonesome George. Lonesome means lonely, which is exactly what poor George was.

> **66** *He came to meet me and . . . stood for a while, with his mouth open, staring at me without blinking, as if he wanted to say something.* **99**
>
> —Fausto Llerena, Lonesome George's keeper

SLOW AND STEADY

The keepers who were caring for him tried to think of a way to make baby Pinta Island tortoises, so that Lonesome George wouldn't be the only one of his kind. But there were no female Pinta Island tortoises left anywhere to become mothers. Instead, they brought two female giant tortoises from another island to live with Lonesome George. The keepers knew that if these tortoises had babies with George, the babies wouldn't be exactly like Pinta Island tortoises, but they would still be keeping George's family tree alive.

Although both female tortoises laid eggs after spending time with him, sadly, none of them hatched. Lonesome George continued to have a slow, steady life, but because he was the only Pinta Island tortoise in the world, he grew very famous. With his long neck, curved shell, and sparkling dark eyes, he became a symbol for conservation, or the protection of wild things and places. He helped people to see how important it is to look after rare animals.

Lonesome George died peacefully in June 2012, 40 years after moving to his new home. We think he was more than 100 years old, which means he lived through two world wars and the invention of the television, the jet engine, and the computer. But it's amazing to think that 100 years old was actually quite young for a Pinta Island tortoise. Scientists think some of them once lived right up to the age of 200!

MAKING HISTORY

When a particular type of animal is gone forever, it is said to have become extinct. Although the world isn't lucky enough to have any Pinta Island tortoises anymore, Lonesome George is still making a difference in the way we think. His body is on display in a special research building in the Galápagos Islands, helping to teach us about conservation. It's always very sad when an animal becomes extinct, but by remembering this gentle giant of a tortoise, we can try to make sure it never happens again.

George at the Charles Darwin Research Station in Ecuador (*above*), and a map of the Galápagos Islands, where George lived (*right*).

66 *This tortoise embodies extinction, quite literally, and people all round the world have been moved by his life, his death, and now his afterlife.* 99

—Henry Nicholls, author of the book *Lonesome George*

CLEVER HANS

The horse who was taught mathematics

WILHELM'S BIG IDEA

For thousands of years, horses have made life easier for humans. They have helped us to travel long distances, to carry heavy loads, and even to plow fields. Horses can do many things very well—but no one ever thought they could do math. That was until a remarkable horse became famous in Germany at the end of the 19th century.

Clever Hans—or "der Kluge Hans," to give him his German name—was a dark young stallion who belonged to a man named Wilhelm von Osten. Wilhelm was a retired schoolteacher who lived in the city of Berlin. But rather than using his horse for riding or for pulling a carriage, he had a very different idea: he wanted to teach Hans how to add and subtract.

When Wilhelm's neighbors saw the horse being shown numbers on a blackboard, they couldn't quite believe what they were seeing. A horse getting math lessons! But this was what happened, day after day, week after week, until in 1891 Wilhelm decided Hans was ready to show people how clever he was.

OLD HORSE, NEW TRICKS

The crowds that came to watch him were amazed by what the horse could do. Wilhelm would give him a problem, and Clever Hans would reply by stamping his front hoof. If the answer was three, he would stamp his hoof three times. He got the answer right every time—and Wilhelm rewarded him with a carrot or piece of sugar every time too. No one had ever seen anything like it—the horse even seemed to understand fractions!

But Clever Hans wasn't just impressing people with math. As his fame grew, Wilhelm taught him new tricks. The horse used his hoof to stamp out the answers to lots of things: the time of day, how much different coins were worth, the colors of different objects, even the month of the year—using one stamp for January, two for February, and so on. This wasn't just a smart animal—this was a miracle! News of the horse's powers even reached the kaiser himself, the emperor of Germany.

Hans with his owner and teacher, Wilhelm von Osten.

But although Hans really was very clever, things were not quite what they seemed. In the early 1900s, a group of 13 experts was asked to study the horse to decide whether he really was some sort of genius. At first they thought it was all true. Clever Hans seemed to know exactly how many times to stamp his hoof, no matter who asked him questions. But then the experts discovered something very important: Hans only got the question right if the person who was asking it knew the answer themselves. And when he was stamping his answers, Hans also had to be able to see the asker.

They realized that, rather than understanding the questions, Clever Hans was actually just very good at watching the asker. This was almost always Wilhelm. The experts noticed that whenever the horse reached the right number of hoof-stamps, Wilhelm would give a small signal without meaning to—his head would move slightly, or his back would straighten. Wilhelm himself didn't even know he was doing this—but the horse did. Clever Hans had become absolutely brilliant at knowing when he was expected to stop stamping.

66 *He possesses the ability to see sharply, to distinguish mental impressions from each other, to retain them in his memory, and to utter them by his hoof language.* **99**
—Professor Möbius, a German zoologist who observed Clever Hans

MAKING HISTORY

More than a hundred years later, scientists and researchers still talk about "the Clever Hans effect" when they're describing stories like this one—when the asker of a question influences the behavior of a person or animal without meaning to. And although this handsome horse may not really have been able to work out math problems, he was very intelligent, very alert—and very good at knowing how to get carrots and sugar!

ELSA

A LITTLE LION

These days, most people understand how important it is that we look after wild animals—that we give them the space they need and the respect they deserve. But it hasn't always been this way. For a long time, people did much less to help wild animals survive, and to protect the places they lived in. Things have changed a lot—and a big part of this is down to an African lioness named Elsa.

In 1956 a wildlife warden named George Adamson was walking across the grassy plains of Kenya when an adult lioness suddenly charged at him. To defend himself, he had to shoot her. Very soon, he understood why she had attacked: the lioness had been protecting her three tiny lion cubs, who were close by. George's house was not far away, so he brought the babies there to keep them safe. He and his wife, Joy, named them Lustica, Big One, and Elsa.

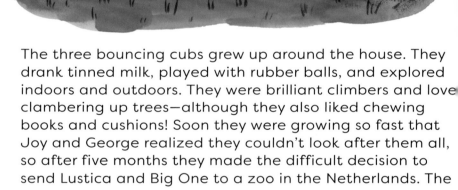

The three bouncing cubs grew up around the house. They drank tinned milk, played with rubber balls, and explored indoors and outdoors. They were brilliant climbers and loved clambering up trees—although they also liked chewing books and cushions! Soon they were growing so fast that Joy and George realized they couldn't look after them all, so after five months they made the difficult decision to send Lustica and Big One to a zoo in the Netherlands. The smallest and liveliest cub, Elsa, stayed with them.

Over the next few years, Elsa went everywhere with Joy and George. She would hop onto the back of their truck, sometimes traveling as far as the sea, where she would play in the waves. She also began to pay more attention to other wild animals on the plains, but because her mother had died when she was so young, she had never been taught how to hunt. Instead Joy had to feed her.

> " Joy was determined to teach Elsa to survive on her own. "
> —BBC Earth

INTO THE WILD

Joy and George understood that Elsa needed a wilder life. They encouraged her to spend time on the plains by herself for days and weeks at a time, hoping that she might meet other lions and learn how to feed herself. Months went by. Elsa was slowly getting used to living like a proper lioness, but she was usually very hungry, and Joy and George still had to give her food.

Then one day, they heard a lot of noise coming from the river. Elsa had caught a buffalo that was crossing the water! It was a clear sign that she was ready to start living on her own in the wild. Joy and George still drove out to the plains to see her from time to time, and less than a year later they spotted her crossing the river again—only this time she wasn't alone. Behind her splashed her three tiny cubs. Elsa was a mother.

> 66 *You can imagine our great joy when a few months later she swam across the river followed by three fine cubs.* 99
> —Joy Adamson, one of the naturalists who took care of Elsa

> 66 *For a few years in the 1960s, Elsa the lioness was the most famous animal alive. Her story . . . inspired thousands of people to become involved in wildlife conservation.* 99
> —BBC Earth

Elsa was the inspiration for a TV series and film version of *Born Free*.

MAKING HISTORY

Joy went on to write three books about Elsa's life, all of which were bestsellers. Two of them were even made into films. But more importantly, Joy's stories had a huge effect on conservation. Elsa inspired thousands of people to help animals that were being harmed or hunted, and in 1984, the actors who played Joy and George in one of the films started the Born Free Foundation, which today helps to look after wildlife around the world.

Elsa was a playful, beautiful lioness, but her life was just the start of a conservation story that's still happening today.

STREETCAT BOB

The stray cat who became a star

A FURRY FRIEND

Animals can make an enormous difference in our lives. They show us love, friendship, and loyalty. They help give us hope when things get tough. They can even change our lives completely. That's what happened in 2007, when James Bowen, a lonely young man living in London, noticed a ginger tomcat sheltering in a hallway. Neither of them could have guessed it at the time, but this was the start of an incredible story—for both James and the cat.

James had a very difficult life. He had no proper home and almost no money. During the day he was a busker—someone who plays music on the street to make a living. At night he slept wherever he could. Sometimes he had to sleep on pavements, or in shop doorways. At other times he stayed in special housing for people who couldn't afford to live anywhere else. This was where he first spotted a tiny cat with a badly injured leg. It looked tired and hungry and didn't seem to belong to anyone.

> **"** *He came to me when he needed help. And I didn't know it then, but I definitely needed the love he gave me. . . . I didn't have anything, and I didn't have anyone, and I didn't have any reason to care, and he gave that to me.* **"**
> —James Bowen, Bob's owner

Three days later the cat was still there. James could see that it needed looking after, so with the little money that he had, he bought some medicine to help it. Before long the cat felt well enough to follow him when he went out. It wanted to be wherever James was. One day it even hopped right onto the Number 73 bus with him! James named his new four-legged friend Bob, and soon they went everywhere together. Suddenly James wasn't so lonely anymore.

FROM THE STREETS TO STARDOM

When James was busking, Bob would sit calmly on a blanket at his feet, or climb up and curl around his neck. In the noise and crowds of central London, people were very surprised and happy to see a man playing the guitar with a ginger cat on his shoulders. Before, James had often been ignored and Bob had just been a stray cat, but now that they were together, the two of them started to become well known. More and more people came to watch them. Some brought little presents for Bob, like knitted scarves and cat treats.

One day, while they were busking, a lady named Mary Pachnos stopped to talk to James. Mary was a literary agent—someone who helps to find ideas for new books—and she asked him if he would be interested in writing about his life with Bob. James had never thought of doing this, but Mary persuaded him to give it a try. Less than a year later, there was a brand-new book in the shops. It had a handsome ginger cat on the cover, and underneath was written *A Street Cat Named Bob*, by James Bowen.

> **"** *It's all down to him. For the first time, I felt like I had family. It gave me the determination to make my life more comfortable, to make his life better, too.* **"**
> —James Bowen

Bob and James at the launch of their bestselling book, *A Street Cat Named Bob*.

MAKING HISTORY

James and Bob became very famous indeed. People loved reading about how the two of them had helped each other, and the book became a bestseller—it was so popular that it was translated into 18 different languages, for readers all around the world. Bob has even had a film made about his life, and now has his own Facebook account, with more than half a million followers!

Life is full of surprises, but no one could have imagined that a busker from London and a stray cat would touch the lives of so many people. Bob's kind nature meant that he now had fans on every continent, but just as importantly, his faithfulness and friendship had changed James's life forever.

> **"** *I owe everything to Bob. We've been on quite a journey together.* **"**
> —James Bowen

SMOKEY

A GROWING DANGER

The forests of North America are full of life. Pine trees crowd the hills, birds fly in the valleys, and silver fish swim in the rivers. Every log, rock, and root hides creepy-crawlies, and all sorts of bigger animals make their homes here too, from deer and foxes to skunks and bears. If you look carefully, you can find dens, nests, and pawprints. But although it's amazing to have so many creatures side by side, there's one thing that can make a forest like this a very dangerous place for animals to be: wildfire.

Wildfire happens when a forest fire gets out of control. This might be because the weather is scorching hot, or because someone has accidentally let a small fire grow bigger. When fire starts to spread, it becomes very difficult to stop. It can cover whole hills and valleys in high, fierce flames, burning everything in its way. This is what happened one summer's day in 1950, in the Capitan Mountains in the United States—and it nearly trapped one very scared black bear cub.

No one knows exactly how the fire started, but by the time it was spotted, it was already sweeping across the land. A hot wind was making the wildfire larger and stronger. The situation was very scary, and when the fire crew arrived, they were told that there was a young cub without its mother, walking around near the fire. He was frightened and confused, but when the fire crew tried to reach him, the flames were too powerful. The crew could only wait.

LUCKY ESCAPE

When they finally found the little bear, they saw that he had climbed up a tall tree to try and escape the wildfire. His paws and legs were badly burned, but incredibly, he was still breathing. One of the crew offered to take him home. His burns were treated and bandaged, and before long, he started to recover.

At first he was given the name Hotfoot Teddy, but this was soon changed. In 1944, the United States Forest Service had introduced a cartoon mascot named Smokey Bear, who taught people about the dangers of fire. This would be the perfect name for a brave cub who had survived such a terrifying experience—so Hotfoot Teddy became the real-life Smokey Bear.

His story soon appeared in newspapers and magazines across the country. The small cub was now famous, and because he had no family to care for him, it was decided that his new home would be the National Zoo in America's capital city, Washington, DC. He traveled on a special private airplane, with an overnight stop at another zoo along the way. And when he arrived in Washington, DC, in June of 1950, hundreds of people were waiting to welcome him, including photographers and groups of Boy and Girl Scouts.

Little Smokey became a celebrity. He spent 26 years living at the zoo, sometimes receiving thousands of letters from children a week! They wrote to say how happy they were that Smokey had been rescued, and to ask if he was okay. Some of them sent him honey, too, and when he wasn't eating his usual food of fruit, vegetables, and fish, he even liked peanut-butter sandwiches.

Smokey playing in his pool at the National Zoo in Washington, DC.

" *Every visitor who came to the zoo had to see Smokey.* **"**
—*The New York Times*

MAKING HISTORY

When Smokey died in 1976, there was only one place he could be taken. His body was flown back to the mountains of New Mexico, to be buried close to the forest where he was first found. He had grown so much that he was almost unrecognizable from the tiny black cub who had desperately climbed a tree all those years ago—but after more than a quarter of a century, Smokey was home again at last.

Smokey appeared on signs to warn people about the danger of forest fires (*above*) and was even turned into a toy (*right*).

MACHLI

The tiger who always defended her cubs

ON THE PROWL

You can sometimes tell a lot about animals by the way they walk. Elephants plod slowly, as if they have all the time in the world. Antelopes step lightly, as if they're rather nervous. And tigers? They move through the jungle like royalty, their alert eyes ahead and their majestic stripes shining. They look as though they're in charge—and one ferocious tiger in the wilds of India showed this attitude more than any other. Her name was Machli, and her courage was famed.

In the northern Indian state of Rajasthan, where the clothes are brightly colored and the cities burst with noise and music, there's also a very big wildlife reserve called Ranthambore National Park. It covers hundreds of square miles with thick forest, sun-baked hills, and crumbling forts. All sorts of wonderful wild animals live here, from monkeys and crocodiles to leopards and tigers. And from the day she was born in the late 1990s, this was Machli's home.

QUEEN OF THE JUNGLE

During the early months of her life, she lived much like other tiger cubs. She learned to hunt, found her way around the jungle, and grew into a strong young animal. As she became a bit older, however, she did something unusual. Adult tigers usually have their own special territory, an area where they live and hunt. In 1999, when Machli was only a few years old but already fierce, she took away part of the park that was controlled by her own mother. Her mother had hunted there before—now it was Machli's territory. It was clear that she would be no ordinary tiger.

The word *machli* means "fish" in the local language, and she was given this name because of the distinctive fish-shaped markings on her face. She was a very beautiful tiger—but she soon became known for far more than her looks. Before long, she started having cubs of her own, and she did everything she could to protect them from harm. Male tigers sometimes attack young cubs, but every time a male came near—even when they were much bigger than her—Machli challenged them angrily and chased them away.

As the years went on, more and more people heard about Machli. She didn't seem to be afraid of anything. Visitors to the park were astonished one day when they saw her in a violent fight with a crocodile at the side of a lake. She probably attacked the crocodile to stop it eating the deer that were close by, because she wanted to eat them herself. But the crocodile was huge—about fourteen feet long! Machli was smaller but much more cunning. She leaped onto its back, pinned it down, and killed it with a fearsome bite to the back of the neck.

> **She defended her cubs from full-grown male tigers, which are significantly bigger. And she won over and over and over.**
>
> —Kalli Doubleday, a carnivore researcher from the University of Texas

MAKING HISTORY

By now, thousands of visitors were coming to try and spot her every year. She appeared in magazines and was shown on TV programs around the world. And even as she grew older and her body began getting weaker, she remained an incredibly powerful mother. Her canine teeth—the sharpest in her mouth—began to fall out, and she lost the use of one of her eyes in a fight with another tiger, but she still went on to raise more cubs and keep them safe!

When she died in 2016, she was around 19 years old, which is an impressive age for a female tiger. The local people were so fond of her that they wanted to give her a special burial, so they wrapped her in a white cloth and placed flowers all over her body. The Indian government even made postage stamps with her face on them. Today, Machli is remembered as far more than just a tiger. She was the brave one-eyed Queen of Ranthambore—a mother who always protected her cubs.

Machli was given the nickname "Tigress Queen of Ranthambore."

KNUT

ROCKY START

Polar bears are very handsome animals. The sight of a fully-grown bear padding slowly over the Arctic ice, thick fur gleaming in the sun, is one of the greatest in the natural world. Today we know a lot about how important it is that we look after these majestic creatures and the places where they live. And thanks to one very special young cub, we also know just how much people care about them.

In December 2006 a female polar bear at Berlin Zoo, Germany, gave birth to two tiny male cubs. Mother bears usually look after their babies, but sometimes—and experts don't completely understand why—they reject them, which means they don't give them the care they need to survive. When the zookeepers saw that the mother was ignoring her cubs, they became worried. Without warmth and food, the little bears would die.

> **"** When Knut was first born, he was no bigger than a snowball. **"**
>
> —from the book *Knut: How One Little Polar Bear Captivated the World*

Knut exploring his enclosure at the Berlin Zoo.

CARING FOR CUBS

Two of the keepers, Thomas and André, decided to look after the cubs themselves. They took them from the enclosure, made a small heated bed for them, and began feeding them milk. Very sadly, one of the young bears lived for only four days, which made Thomas and André even more determined to keep the other cub safe and healthy. He had bright black eyes and soft white fur. They named him Knut (pronounced K'-noot).

Caring for Knut took a lot of time. The cub needed feeding every few hours, so Thomas made sure he was always close by. He gave Knut baths, kept his bed toasty warm, and even slept in the same room. The bear grew fluffier, stronger, and more curious about the world around him. He liked pouncing on his soft toys and play-wrestling with Thomas. Stories of the lively cub started appearing in the newspapers, and people loved reading about how well the little animal was doing. He even had his own nickname: "Cute K'noot"!

Visitors to the zoo were eager to see Knut for themselves, but he was still a very young bear. The keepers wanted to make sure the cub would only appear in public once he was ready. Eventually, when he was nearly four months old, he was shown to visitors for the first time. Thousands of people and TV cameras from all around the world were there to see him, and within a few days the adorable little bear had become a global star.

Knut received big bags of letters every week—poems, messages, and drawings from his new fans—and the zoo became busier and busier whenever he was taken outside. Children bought special Knut cuddly toys, and coins and stamps with the bear's picture were made. Soon the cub even had his own TV series!

MAKING HISTORY

Thomas looked after Knut, but as the young bear grew bigger and more independent, the keeper stayed with him less and less. Knut ate lots of fish and meat, and as the years passed by he became a very impressive-looking bear. He lived at the zoo for the rest of his life, always drawing big crowds. Today a statue of Knut still stands in Berlin Zoo, showing him relaxing on a rock.

Knut was noble, playful, and full of character, but even as a cub he was far more than just a cute attraction. He also reminded millions of people that polar bears are extraordinary animals, needing all the care and protection that we can give.

Did you know?

Wild polar bears usually live on and around sea ice in the Arctic Circle. Climate change, or global warming, is slowly melting this ice. It's hugely important that we humans do what we can to help polar bears keep their home.

A polar bear and her cub on the drifting sea ice.

CHRISTIAN

FROM HARRODS TO HOME

In the middle of London, England, there stands a large department store called Harrods. It sells all sorts of interesting things, from luxury chocolates to million-dollar watches. In 1969, however, it had something more unusual for sale: a lion cub. The little animal had been bought from a zoo and was now living in a cage in the Harrods pet department, next to the kittens and the sheepdogs.

When two young men named John Rendall and Ace Bourke visited the store one day, they were shocked when they saw the cub in its cage. Their friends told them it would be a bad idea to buy a lion, but this only made them more determined. Before long, John and Ace had a new roommate with golden fur, sharp teeth, and four paws. They named him Christian.

Their friend Derek took photographs of Christian, with John and Ace, getting up to all sorts of tricks.

❝ Christian changed the path of our lives. ❞

—John Rendall, one of Christian's owners

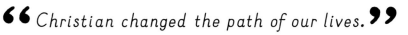

For the first few months, John and Ace looked after Christian as if he were a puppy. They fed him, play-wrestled with him, and let him sleep on their beds. Sometimes they even drove him to the seaside. He soon grew too big for the apartment, so they moved him to the furniture store they worked in, turning part of it into a den for Christian. Imagine the surprise their customers got when they saw a snoozing lion on the floor!

LEAVING LONDON

John and Ace loved Christian, and Christian was very fond of them, too. The playful lion would often jump into their arms and give them slobbery licks. But they understood that if Christian was going to live like a true lion when he was fully grown, he needed to be in the wild. It was a very difficult decision, but they knew it was best for Christian, so they got in touch with George Adamson, who lived in an African country called Kenya. (You can read more about George in Elsa's story on page 50.)

George agreed to help introduce Christian to the wild—although it wouldn't be easy. Christian had never hunted for his food before, so they knew that if he was going to survive, he would need to be part of a pride, or group of lions.

It took time, but eventually Christian found a pride in Kenya where he was safe and accepted. He began a new life in the wild and was seen only occasionally by humans. George wrote to John and Ace in London to let them know that Christian was now much bigger and had a family of his own, which made the two men very happy. So happy, in fact, that they decided to go back to Kenya see their old pet one last time.

> **66** *We called him and he stood up and started to walk toward us very slowly. Then, as if he had become convinced it was us, he ran toward us, threw himself onto us, knocked us over . . . and hugged us, like he used to, with his paws on our shoulders.* **99**
>
> —John Rendall

MAKING HISTORY

When John and Ace arrived at the nature reserve in Kenya, they thought it would be difficult to find Christian, but soon a familiar-looking lion appeared in the hills. They called his name. It had been a year since they'd last seen each other, and Christian approached slowly. Then he recognized them and, with an excited scamper, ran forward, leaped on top of them, and gave them both big lion hugs!

Christian hadn't forgotten his friends, even after living in Kenya for over a year.

It was a beautiful moment. Even Christian's lioness came over to be stroked. Christian's amazing life highlighted something very important: lions deserve all the care that we can give them.

ENDAL

The dog who saved his owner's life

ASSISTANCE DOG

A FRIEND IN NEED

All dogs are different, but sometimes we hear about a dog who is one in a million. This is how we can describe Endal, a dog who did all sorts of amazing things—and changed his owner's life forever.

Endal was a yellow Labrador retriever who lived in England. He was born in 1995, and when he was still young, he was trained as an assistance dog, which is a dog that helps look after humans who have disabilities. Even though Endal had a disease which meant his own legs were often stiff, he was still enthusiastic about doing the things that a good assistance dog had to do. He was clever and eager and could solve problems—all of which was excellent news for Allen Parton, the man who would become his owner.

Before he met Endal, life was very difficult for Allen. In 1991 he had been a navy officer in the Gulf War, where he was badly hurt. Back in England, he needed to use a wheelchair, and his injuries also meant he couldn't talk or remember things properly, which made him sad and frustrated. Then one day he went with his wife to the dog-training center where she worked. A young dog came up to him, licked his hands, and stayed by his side. It was Endal.

SAVING THE DAY

Before long, it was decided that Endal would live with Allen and help him with the tasks he found tricky. The dog was only a few years old but could already do things like empty clothes from the washing machine, mail letters, and help to get money out of a cash machine! Having a bright and helpful companion like Endal made Allen much happier—and soon his new friend would also save his life.

> ❝ *Having a thinking and problem-solving dog at my side makes anything possible.* ❞
> —Allen Parton, Endal's owner

One dark evening in 2001, Allen and Endal were going along the pavement when they were hit by a speeding car. Allen was knocked out of his wheelchair and banged his head. Endal knew exactly what to do. He moved Allen into a position where he could breathe easily, covered him with a blanket, and then ran to a nearby hotel, barking to attract attention. The dog's quick thinking meant Allen could be taken to the hospital right away.

This incredible event brought Endal and Allen even closer. By now the dog understood more than 100 different hand signals—when Allen touched his head, for example, Endal knew he needed his hat—and could do lots of extraordinary things. He could fetch newspapers, pick up telephones, hand over bank cards in shops, and open train doors. He even knew how to pull out the plug from a bathtub!

> ❝ *Until I met him, I was in the depths of despair. But when he refused to leave my side at the training center, I suddenly saw a chink of light.* ❞
> —Allen Parton

Allen with Endal wearing his PDSA Gold Medal for Animal Gallantry and Devotion to Duty, the highest award an animal can be given.

MAKING HISTORY

Unsurprisingly, Endal was now a star. He was given the PDSA Gold Medal, a very special award for animal bravery, to reward his behavior when Allen was hit by the car. He won lots of other awards too, including being voted Dog of the Millennium! Television crews from around the world came to film him; Allen and his wife wrote a book about how much he had helped them; and a road near their house was even named Endal Way in his honor. He also became the first-ever dog to ride the London Eye Ferris wheel.

When Endal died in 2009, the world lost an assistance dog whose devotion had completely turned his owner's life around and inspired many others. Like all Labrador retrievers, he liked going for walks, eating treats, and being patted, but Endal was also brainy, courageous—and a truly awesome companion.

SAM

The koala who survived a wildfire

Terrifying wildfires burning the forests in Victoria, Australia.

A NATURAL DISASTER

Australia's wildlife comes in all shapes and sizes, from bouncy kangaroos and waddling wombats to giant crocodiles and brightly feathered cockatoos. The country is also home to one of the most recognizable creatures in the world—a fluffy-eared, leaf-eating bundle of fur that spends almost all its time asleep up a tree. It is, of course, the adorable koala, an animal that lives only in the woodlands of Australia.

A koala's life is usually a relaxed one. When it's not dozing, it can normally be found chomping on eucalyptus leaves or moving slowly through the branches. But sometimes disaster strikes. This was what happened in the hot summer of 2009, when the sun became so strong that a huge area of woodland in Victoria, in the south of the country, caught fire. Fierce flames raced quickly through the dry forest, destroying nearby homes and swallowing up trees. It was the worst fire that this part of Australia had ever seen.

ESCAPE FROM THE FLAMES

It was incredibly dangerous, both for the people who lived close by and the many different animals that lived in the woodland. As the fire grew bigger and more out of control, many lost their lives, while many more had to do what they could to escape the terrible flames. Wallabies hopped, snakes slithered, and birds flew, while hundreds of firefighters worked day and night to try and put out the fire.

It was one of these firefighters who found the hero of this story. In a quiet area of forest, a firefighter named Dave Tree was walking through the blackened trees when he spotted an animal by itself: a young female koala. She had somehow survived the flames, but she was exhausted, confused, and scared. Her paws were badly burned and she was weak and very thirsty. Dave could see that the wild animal needed help, so he spoke to her gently and held out a bottle of water for her to drink. She guzzled it so quickly that he had to give her another one!

64

It was clear that the koala would have to go somewhere safe, so she was taken to a local wildlife shelter, where they named her Sam. When the newspapers heard about Sam being rescued, her story appeared all over the world, helping to give people a feeling of hope after the awful news of the fire. She might have just been a small animal, but because of what had happened to her, she became an important symbol of survival.

Lots of injured koalas like Sam were rescued, helped to recover, and then released back into the wild.

"She is lovely—very docile—and she has already got an admirer. A male koala keeps putting his arms around her."
—Jenny Shaw, a carer at the wildlife shelter

MAKING HISTORY

And Sam wasn't the only koala at the shelter. A male koala named Bob had also been rescued from the fire, and the two of them were able to begin their recovery together. Their friendship gave people something cheerful to think about at a very difficult time. Sam gave us a further surprise too. When international pop stars released a collection of songs to raise money for the victims of the fire, the photo on the cover was very special: it showed Dave feeding water to Sam. The wildfire will never be forgotten, and neither will Sam. Australia is a country full of amazing creatures, and thanks to one young koala, we'll always remember just how brave they can be.

DOLLY

The sheep who was a breakthrough for science

A SPECIAL SHEEP

When Dolly the sheep was born in Scotland in 1996, she looked and acted like any other young lamb. She had a white fleece and bright eyes and was curious about the world around her. But there was something very special about Dolly. Rather than having a mother and father, like most lambs, she had been created with the help of human scientists and three different female sheep, or ewes. Dolly was an exact copy—a clone—of one of these ewes, so her story is an amazing one.

To understand how she was born, it's helpful to think of Dolly as having three mothers and no father. She was "built" when scientists took a tiny piece of body tissue—called a cell, and far smaller than even a grain of sand—from the udder of her first mother. Dolly would become a clone of this sheep.

The scientists then removed an egg from her second mother, and joined the cell and egg together. This created a sheep embryo, the very beginnings of a baby lamb, which was placed inside her third mother. Then the scientists waite

HELLO, DOLLY

After 148 days, having grown inside the sheep just like a normal lamb, Dolly was born. She was a small, bleating bundle of wool with wobbly legs—but she was soon to become world-famous. It was the first time that a mammal had ever been cloned from an adult cell. Other scientists had tried to do the same for decades, without success, so when Dolly's birth was announced, people were astonished.

> **❝** It's unbelievable. It basically means that there are no limits. It means all of science fiction is true. They said it could never be done and now here it is, done before the year 2000. **❞**
>
> —Dr. Lee Silver, a biology professor at Princeton University, speaking about Dolly's birth in 1997

> **"** *Dolly Parton said she was 'honored' that we have named our progeny after her and that there is no such thing as 'baaaaad publicity.'* **"**
>
> —Harry Griffin, a scientist at the Roslin Institute in Scotland, where Dolly was born

A sweater made from Dolly's wool, as part of a competition called "Do a Design for Dolly."

Many of them thought Dolly's birth was a brilliant achievement, a triumph for science that would help us understand more about the way cells work. But others thought it was wrong to create an animal in this way. Some began wondering whether one day it might be possible to clone humans.

Within just a week, the institute where Dolly was born received 3,000 phone calls from around the world. She was named after Dolly Parton, a very popular country singer, and for a while she was just as famous. Stories about Dolly the sheep appeared in newspapers and magazines, film crews rushed to record pictures of her, and she quickly became the most photographed sheep of all time.

As Dolly grew up, the scientists were pleased to see that in lots of ways she was a normal sheep. Her brain, heart, and other organs all worked properly, and she lived an active life with the other sheep at the institute. She even became a mother herself, having six baby lambs with a mountain ram. After developing a problem with her lungs, she died in 2003, at the age of six. Today her body is still on display at the National Museum of Scotland in Edinburgh.

Thousands of people visit Dolly's body every year.

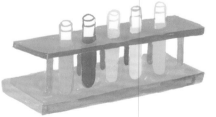

MAKING HISTORY

Because of Dolly, scientists were then able to clone other animals in the same way. Horses, pigs, goats, rats, mice, dogs, mules, and even monkeys have all now been born using "the Dolly method."

Sometimes animals can have a huge impact on the world without ever knowing anything about it. Dolly is a classic example: the famous Scottish sheep who made a giant scientific leap.

DAVID GREYBEARD

The chimpanzee who learned to trust humans

CURIOUS CHIMPANZEE

When a young British woman named Jane Goodall traveled to Tanzania in 1960 to learn more about chimpanzees, it wasn't an easy time for her. She was a primatologist, an expert on apes and monkeys. But the chimpanzees were difficult for Jane to find in the thick African jungle, and whenever she did manage to spot them, they ran away or swung off through the trees.

Then one day, instead of disappearing into the forest, one chimpanzee stayed calmly where he was, letting Jane watch him and come close to where he was sitting. He had gray hairs on his chin and was as curious about Jane as she was about him. Jane named this chimpanzee David Greybeard.

TRUST AND TOOLS

Back then, people didn't know as much about chimpanzees as we do now. Jane was one of the first scientists to study them in the wild, and over the years she has shown us how clever, creative, and loyal these animals can be. For this we can thank David Greybeard, who was the first chimpanzee to trust Jane. When the others saw that he was comfortable being close to her—and that she was peaceful—they lost their fear of being near her too.

Wild chimpanzees had always avoided humans before, but David Greybeard let Jane touch him and clean his fur. He became so relaxed around her that he even stole bananas from her tent. But he wasn't just a trusting chimpanzee—he was also caring, playful, and very intelligent. No animal on the planet has more in common with humans than the chimpanzee, and David Greybeard helped us to see this.

Jane noticed how he would often comfort his friend Goliath by resting a hand on his head or body. Once, when she offered him a red palm nut, a fruit from the jungle, David Greybeard gently brushed it away but looked her in the eyes and gave her hand a soft squeeze. It was his way of saying thank you.

He was also the first chimpanzee that Jane saw using a tool. He was holding a long, thin piece of grass and dipping it into a termite mound, or insect nest. Every time he brought the grass back out there were insects on it, which David Greybeard ate. He was using the grass to "fish" for food. This was a hugely exciting discovery for Jane. Before this moment, people thought that humans were the only creatures clever enough to make and use tools.

Jane describes David Greybeard as handsome and kind, but like all wild animals, he did what he had to do to survive. We used to think chimpanzees ate only fruits and leaves, so when Jane saw him chewing on the flesh of a recently killed baby bush pig, it was the first time we learned that they also sometimes ate meat.

David was the first chimpanzee Jane saw using tools, which was a very important discovery.

MAKING HISTORY

David Greybeard was already an adult when Jane arrived in Tanzania, and he lived for a further eight years. But Jane's work continued, as did her love for animals. Many decades later, having studied hundreds of wild chimpanzees over more than half a century, she still speaks of David Greybeard as her all-time favorite. And without him, perhaps we would all be unaware of just how special chimpanzees can be.

66 *He was the very first chimpanzee who let me come close, who lost his fear ... The other chimps would see David sitting there not running away and so gradually they'd think, 'Well, she can't be so scary after all.' ... He had a wonderful gentle disposition; he was really loved by other chimps.* 99

—Jane Goodall, the primatologist who studied David Greybeard

David and Jane formed a bond that lasted a lifetime.

ALEX

PET SHOP PARROT

If we call someone a "birdbrain," it usually means they're not being very clever. But thanks to an African gray parrot, we now know that a bird's brain can do incredible things. In the 30 years he was alive, he learned to speak 150 English words, could recognize different colors, and could even ask for different foods—and all this with a brain that was only as big as a walnut! His name was Alex, and he was an extraordinary parrot.

Alex wasn't a wild bird. Even though he was an African gray, he probably wasn't born in Africa. And when he was bought from a pet shop in Chicago in 1977 by Dr. Irene Pepperberg, he was only about a year old. Irene worked in a university as an ethologist, someone who studies animal behavior, and she wanted to do some experiments with a bird. She didn't know it at the time, but she had just bought a very special one.

She named him Alex, a name short for Avian Learning Experiment (avian means having to do with birds). Parrots are excellent mimics, or copiers, and people have known for a long time that they can repeat some words and noises when they hear them. But Irene was trying to do something different. She wanted to see if parrots could actually understand what they were saying. And as Alex got used to his new home at Irene's university, something very impressive started to happen.

> **❝ Sometimes a single individual changes the world, even if it is a parrot. ❞**
> —Frans de Waal, a Dutch ethologist

Irene began training Alex to recognize different objects and to learn how to ask for things. One way she did this was to show him a person asking for a small treat, like a grape. Alex didn't understand at first, but after watching and listening several times, he began to realize what he needed to say to get the treat. And as his training continued, he got better and better at using different words.

NOT JUST A BIRDBRAIN

After a while, he could call certain objects by their names: things like "key," "paper," and "cork." He could also recognize some of the different colors. He could even put the words together, saying, for example, "Green cork." If he wanted to play with it, he would say, "Want cork." He could count up to six, and sometimes he put words together to describe things in different ways. If he was shown a triangle, he would say, "Three corner."

Alex didn't get the objects and colors right every single time, but soon he knew so many words that he and Irene could almost have a full conversation. He could say, "Come here" and, when he was bored with his lessons, "Wanna go." He could also say "no," and used the word when he was given bits of food that he thought were too small! He grew very attached to Irene and even became jealous when she paid attention to other birds.

> 66 *Clearly, animals know more than we think, and think a great deal more than we know.* 99
> —Dr. Irene Pepperberg, who studied Alex

MAKING HISTORY

Alex died in 2007, when he was 31. He never knew what it was like to live free, but he taught us a huge amount about how amazing birds can be. His last words before he died were to Irene, when she left him at the end of the day. As she opened the door to go and wished him good night, he said, "You be good. I love you."

> 66 *I took care of Alex ... but he was such a free spirit that I never felt I owned him.* 99
> —Dr. Irene Pepperberg

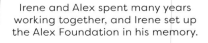

Irene and Alex spent many years working together, and Irene set up the Alex Foundation in his memory.

KOKO

SPECIAL CONNECTION

Gorillas are astonishing animals. They're big, hairy, and enormously strong, but they're also patient, caring, and highly intelligent. If you ever have the chance to look at one close up and see it staring back at you, brown eyes shining, you'll understand why people feel such a deep connection to them. Gorillas usually live in the wild green rain forests of central Africa, but some have to spend their lives in zoos or research centers instead. This is how one unforgettable gorilla became well known around the world.

In 1971 a baby western lowland gorilla was born in the San Francisco Zoo. The zookeepers named her Hanabiko, or Koko for short. She was a small bundle of black fur with floppy arms and a big appetite. When she was just a few months old, she was visited by Penny Patterson, a student trying to discover more about gorilla behavior.

Penny wanted to see if it was possible to teach a gorilla how to use sign language, a way of communicating using hand signs, and she soon realized that young Koko was an excellent learner.

A GREAT APE

Penny started by showing the baby gorilla some simple signs for "eat," "drink," and "more." When Koko seemed to understand and use these hand signs, Penny taught her some more. Koko became so good at learning new signs that in 1974 she was moved from the zoo to the university where Penny worked. And as the years went on and Koko grew larger, the number of different words she could sign grew and grew. People could hardly believe it was possible—a gorilla that could use its hands to talk with humans!

> **"** Sign language . . . has allowed both Koko and me to express our feelings, to prevent misunderstandings, and to reassure ourselves of the other's affection and trust. **"**
>
> —Dr. Francine "Penny" Patterson, who studied Koko

Penny had planned to work with Koko for just four years, but she became so fond of the gorilla that they stayed together for more than 40. By the time Koko was fully grown, she could understand around 2,000 spoken words and use more than 1,000 different hand signs for things like "flower," "love," "sorry," "surprise," and "polite." She was even able to use these hand signs to make short sentences—"bring me cat," for example—and sometimes to invent her own words, like "finger bracelet" for "ring" or "scratch comb" for "brush."

Her sign language amazed people across the world, and for many years she appeared on TV programs and in magazines. Once, the front page of *National Geographic* magazine even showed a photo that Koko had taken of herself in the mirror!

MAKING HISTORY

But Koko was much more than just a gorilla who could use sign language. She was funny, loving, cheeky, and kind. Her life was very different from the natural life of a wild animal, but she taught us a huge amount about how gorillas think. She loved being tickled, got unhappy when she watched sad films, and became excited every year when Penny gave her a birthday party—complete with

cake and candles. She played with toys and adored having pet kittens, which she would gently pick up to cuddle and stroke. Koko's favorite kitten was named All Ball, and Penny even wrote a children's book about the two animals called *Koko's Kitten*.

Some people thought it was wrong for a gorilla to live like Koko did, and not everyone believed that she could do all the things Penny said she could do. But when Koko died in her sleep in 2018, the world remembered an incredible animal who had shown us just how clever a great ape can be. She had been an inspiration to many people and a true friend to Penny—but she also completely changed the way we think about gorillas.

> 66 *Koko touched the lives of millions . . . She was beloved and will be deeply missed.* 99
> —The Gorilla Foundation

Koko giving the "to listen" sign in sign language, telling Penny she wants to listen to the phone.

PICKLES

The dog who found the World Cup

PUPPIES AND PRIZES

The soccer World Cup is one of the most exciting sports competitions on earth. Held every four years, it's a big event where the best teams from every continent try to become the world champions. It's noisy, colorful, and dramatic, with millions of fans and lots of fast, skillful players. But can you imagine how they would all feel if the prize—the World Cup trophy itself—went missing? That's exactly what happened in England in 1966, and without the help of a clever collie dog named Pickles, it might have been lost forever.

Pickles was born in the early 1960s. He was an energetic little puppy with perky ears, black patches, and a bright, curious nature—and he loved chewing furniture! His owner, John Corbett, found it very tiring to look after Pickles, so John's brother David agreed to take care of the puppy instead. David was a lighterman—someone who worked with ships on the River Thames—and he enjoyed taking Pickles on long walks near his home in south London.

But it wasn't until 1966 that Pickles's story really began. It was a very special time for England. The World Cup was being held in the country for the first time ever, and four months before the competition began, the World Cup trophy, known as the Jules Rimet Trophy, was on display in central London. Many people came to admire its beautiful design, which showed a Greek goddess decorated in gold. The trophy always had guards around it, but one day they got distracted—and while the guards looked the other way, the trophy disappeared. Someone had stolen the World Cup!

WORLD CUP
TROPHY
STOLEN

REWARD OFFERED

MISSING FROM LONDON
STAMP EXHIBITION

A LUCKY DISCOVERY

This was a disaster. The world's best soccer players would soon be arriving in England, but the prize they were trying to win had vanished—and no one knew who had taken it. For a week, the police hunted high and low. Every time they thought they had a clue, it led them nowhere. No one knew where to look. Meanwhile, a small black-and-white dog with a red collar and bundles of energy was about to come to the rescue.

> " Police at Scotland Yard took control of the investigation but had few leads. "
> —BBC report

74

> **"** *Pickles began the life of a celebrity.* **"**
> —The Guardian

Seven days after the theft, David was taking Pickles out for his usual Sunday evening walk when he noticed the dog sniffing around excitedly behind a car next to a hedge. David tried to call him away, but Pickles kept returning to the car. And when David went to see what the dog was doing, he saw something very strange—Pickles had found a package hidden behind the front wheel. It was quite big, quite heavy, and wrapped in newspaper. What could it be?

MAKING HISTORY

When David tore open part of the package to have a look, he couldn't believe what he was seeing. It was the World Cup! He and Pickles went straight to the police station to hand it in. No one ever discovered exactly who stole the trophy, but as soon as people found out what had happened, Pickles became an international hero. He appeared on TV and had his picture in all the newspapers. He was even named Dog of the Year and given a year's supply of free dog food!

But the best was still to come. When England actually won the trophy four months later, Pickles and David were invited to the winners' banquet to celebrate. The players made a special fuss of Pickles—he was given a medal, a silver bowl, and a new rubber bone to chew. But the real highlight? He was allowed to lick David's dinner plate clean!

South London police announcing the safe return of the World Cup trophy (*top*), and Pickles wearing a medal that was presented to him as a reward (*bottom*).

ROY & SILO

The penguins who did things their way

FAR FROM HOME

Have you ever seen the film *Madagascar*? If you have, you'll know that the animals begin their journey at a zoo in the middle of New York City. This is Central Park Zoo, a real zoo with creatures from around the world. It has sea lions, snow leopards, and slithering snakes—and just like in the film, it has penguins, too. It's strange to see penguins so far from where they normally live, and the zoo always has to make sure they have enough water to swim in and enough fish to eat.

There are different kinds of penguins at the zoo—some are big and some are small. The smallest ones are called chinstrap penguins. These cute, waddling little birds take their name from the black stripes under their beaks, which look a bit like hat straps. They're usually found at the very bottom of the world in the seas around Antarctica, but in New York they have so many visitors that some of them become famous. This story is about two chinstrap penguins who did exactly that. Their names were Roy and Silo.

PENGUIN PARTNERS

When chinstrap penguins find a partner, it normally means a male bird and a female bird getting together. Roy and Silo were partners—but they were a bit different. In the six years from 1998 to 2004 they did almost everything together. They built a nest together, swam together, and curled their necks together to show how much they cared for each other. Like all penguin couples, they had a very special bond. But there was one thing that made them even more interesting. They were both male.

Central Park Zoo (*above and left*) is home to four species of penguin: king penguins, rockhopper penguins, gentoo penguins, and chinstrap penguins, like Roy and Silo.

This didn't stop them living like other penguins. When Roy and Silo saw penguin couples hatching eggs, they even tried to do the same themselves. They discovered an egg-shaped rock and sat on it to keep it safe and warm. The zookeepers noticed this, so when a different penguin couple had an egg that they couldn't look after, the keepers gave it to Roy and Silo instead.

> 66 *They tried to incubate a rock together in 1999, so a year later the couple was given an extra egg from another pair. Tango, a female, hatched later that spring.* 99
> —The New York Times

The two penguins did a wonderful job of protecting the egg in their nest. They made sure it was always cared for and took turns sitting on it. They did so well that a few weeks later a penguin chick was born—a tiny ball of gray feathers with a little black beak. Roy and Silo had a baby!

MAKING HISTORY

They fed her, nuzzled her, and taught her how to let them know when she was hungry. Unlike most other penguin chicks, she had two fathers to look after her. The zookeepers named the chick Tango, and when people heard about the new penguin family in the zoo, Roy, Silo, and Tango became famous. Lots of people came to see the three of them, and they even had a picture book written about their lives.

Chinstrap penguins are fascinating birds. Every year, millions of them nest, feed, and swim in the faraway cold of the polar regions—but it was two penguins in the middle of New York City who showed just how much they can surprise us.

OZY

The octopus who could open a jar in seconds

CURIOUS CREATURE

Not many creatures on the planet are as strange or interesting as an octopus. It has two eyes and one pair of jaws, which is normal enough, but after that things start getting rather peculiar. Its brain is wrapped around its throat and shaped like a doughnut. It has not one, not two, but three hearts. It has blue blood, squirts out ink when it senses danger, and as for its arms—well, let's just say it has more than seven and fewer than nine, which is quite enough for any animal to be getting on with.

Eight arms! Just imagine all the things that could be done with eight arms—particularly by a creature as intelligent as an octopus. Because one thing we know for certain is that octopuses are supersmart. They might not have bones, but they have brainpower. So much brainpower, in fact, that marine researchers, people who study underwater life, are still being amazed by the things these incredible animals can do. And this is where an octopus named Ozy joins the story.

Octopuses live in oceans all over the world.

> *Ozy glided up to the jar. He delicately touched it with one of his arms. Then, in a flash, he leaped on top of it.*
> —Judy Hutt, from Island Bay Marine Education Centre

BRAIN TRAINING

In November 2013, fishermen brought an injured octopus to the Island Bay Marine Education Centre in Wellington, New Zealand. They thought it might have been attacked by an eel because one of its arms had been badly hurt. The helpers at the center named the octopus Ozymandias, or Ozy for short. They wanted to help the octopus get better again, so it could be released back into the wild.

When octopuses like Ozy are kept in captivity—in a center like this one, for example—the helpers don't always simply give them food. Sometimes the octopuses' meals are put in places that are tricky to reach, such as hidden along a series of underwater tunnels or shut in different kinds of containers. This isn't to be cruel. It's to keep the octopuses' brains active and to copy how they would hunt for food in the sea, where they often have to move rocks or squeeze into gaps to find something to eat.

MAKING HISTORY

The staff at the center soon discovered that Ozy was very good at getting his food—far better, in fact, than anyone could have imagined. When the helpers gave him a purple shore crab shut tightly inside a large screw-top jar, they knew he would probably be able to open it if they gave him enough time. Octopuses had used their long, strong arms to open jars like this before, spending a few minutes working out how to get the tops off. But clever Ozy didn't need a few minutes—he unscrewed the jar and was gobbling up his crab breakfast in just 54 seconds!

Ozy's speedy jar-opening made headlines around the world, giving yet another reason for people to be amazed by the eight-armed masterminds of the ocean. Octopuses have lived on earth for millions and millions of years—but, incredibly, they still have the power to surprise us.

PAUL

Octopuses have done all sorts of remarkable things. In 2010, an octopus named Paul "predicted" the World Cup results of the German soccer team by choosing food from one of two boxes before each game—one marked with the German flag, the other with the flag of the country they were about to play. He chose the box of the winning country seven times out of seven. A clever power, or just a coincidence?

Paul the octopus correctly predicted the winners of the seven FIFA World Cup matches Germany played in 2010.

NIM CHIMPSKY

The chimpanzee raised as a human

CHIMP OR CHILD

Sometimes stories can fascinate us and make us sad at the same time. This is a good way to think about the life of Nim Chimpsky, a playful chimpanzee who lived in the United States. Chimpanzees are usually only found in Africa, so right from the start, Nim's life was out of the ordinary. He lived to the age of 26, and he spent every one of those years being looked after by humans. His story involves no jungles, no tropical heat, and no swinging through the branches, but it very much deserves to be told.

Nim playing with a piece
of chalk and slate.

Nim was born in 1973 in Oklahoma at the Institute for Primate Studies, a place where scientists study apes and monkeys, and he was taken away from his mother when he was just ten days old. The young animal was then flown to Columbia University in New York, where researchers wanted to see if a chimpanzee could learn how to use sign language.

> 66 *This extraordinary being and I lived our ordinary lives together.* 99
> —Laura-Ann Petitto, one of the scientists who studied Nim

Their plan was to treat him almost as if he were a human child. They named him Nim Chimpsky—a jokey name that sounded like the name of a famous language expert, Noam Chomsky—and he was taken to stay with a local family. Here in New York, among seven human children, he began a new life. He was made to wear sweaters, T-shirts, and shorts, and he ate at the table with the rest of the family. He even had his own toothbrush and slept in a bed.

LEARNING TO SIGN

Nim lived like this for two years. He started to learn different hand signs for words like "eat," "hug," and "sorry." Because he was a chimpanzee, he also did things he wasn't supposed to. He pulled piles of books from the shelves, jumped headfirst into bowls of food, and often refused to brush his teeth. He became harder and harder to control, so he was taken to live at the university. Nim still had his own bedroom and spent his days with humans, but his life was calmer.

While he was here, he learned more hand signs. By the third year of the project, he knew 128 different signs and could use them to say things like "banana Nim eat," "tickle me Nim play," and "give orange me." But in 1977, almost four years after the researchers had begun their project, Nim was becoming too strong and difficult to look after. He often bit people dangerously hard—sometimes even when he was playing—so they decided that the project had to end.

PLAY

HUG

EAT

> *Many (people) are still under the spell of his legendary charm, mischievous sense of humor, and keen understanding of human beings.*
>
> —from the book *Nim Chimpsky: The Chimp Who Would Be Human*

Nim spent the rest of his life in other research centers, first back in Oklahoma—where he slept in a cage but could also spend time with other chimps—then at a medical laboratory, where he would have been very unhappy. People were sad to see Nim being treated in this way, so in 1983 he was moved again, this time to an animal sanctuary. It was here that he spent the last 17 years of his life, before dying naturally in the year 2000.

MAKING HISTORY

Many books, films, and stories have been written about Nim. For a long time he was the most famous chimpanzee in the world, and a lot of the things he did were amazing for us to see. He loved playing with cats, riding in strollers, and being tickled, and his favorite hand signs were always the ones for "play" and "eat." His intelligence also taught us a lot about the way that apes think. And although his life was a very unusual one, Nim Chimpsky showed us something very important: you can't stop a chimpanzee being a chimpanzee—which is exactly how it should be.

A documentary film came out in 2011 (*right*) about Nim's life and the humans who raised him (*below*).

WINTER

The dolphin with a special tail

TROUBLE AT SEA

Dolphins are wonderful swimmers. They speed through the sea, twisting and turning one moment and leaping above the waves the next. Their amazing agility is all thanks to their powerful tails, which they use to steer and propel themselves. Without a tail, it would be much harder for a dolphin to move around underwater—which is why one extraordinary bottlenose dolphin named Winter has become so famous.

> ❝ *You could tell she still had a lot of energy and fight left in her.* ❞
> —Teresa Mazza, the aquarium researcher who rescued Winter

Winter was only two months old when she was found tangled up in a crab net on the coast of Florida in 2005. It was a cold December day, which is how she eventually got her name. Poor Winter was completely stuck, and her tail had become so badly trapped in the net that her blood flow was cut off. A team of experts took the baby dolphin to a local aquarium, where they tried to get her healthy again, but they found it impossible to mend her tail. They decided that to help Winter, the tail would have to be amputated, or cut off.

LEARNING TO SWIM AGAIN

The problem now, of course, was that she found it difficult to swim properly. She only had a stump where her tail had been, and she needed to swish it from side to side to move around the aquarium pool. It was tiring for such a young dolphin, and bad for her spine, so the experts came up with another idea. They wanted to make a brand-new tail for Winter!

A specialist named Kevin Carroll started working on a model tail for her. Kevin had lots of experience in making replacement body parts, or prosthetics, for animals like dogs and birds. But he soon found that creating a new tail for a bottlenose dolphin was much more complicated, because it needed to move in every direction.

" *As she glides through the water, Winter the dolphin appears to be completely normal. But she is the world's first bionic sea creature after being fitted with an artificial tail.* **"**
—*The Daily Telegraph*

After more than a year of trying, Kevin managed to design a tail that he hoped would work. It was made of silicone and plastic, with two flukes at the end just like a normal dolphin tail. But would Winter be able to swim with it? Things didn't get off to a good start. When it was first attached to her, she didn't understand what it was and shook it off again. The team at the aquarium stayed patient, and slowly but surely, the dolphin began to realize that the new tail was there to help her. Eventually she started moving it up and down, up and down, up and down. Kevin and the team were delighted. Winter was swimming properly again!

Winter's prosthetic tail, which helps her to swim.

Winter swimming in Clearwater Marine Aquarium, Florida.

MAKING HISTORY

Once she got the hang of it, Winter started gliding around her pool as playfully and gracefully as a dolphin in the sea. She was swimming well, eating lots of fish—and fast becoming a celebrity, too. Millions of people heard Winter's story on the news, and she helped bring hope to people who had their own difficulties to overcome. She even had a Hollywood film made about her rescue and recovery, with Winter herself in the starring role.

She was just a young dolphin when she was found tangled up on the Florida coastline, and we can only imagine how scary and confusing the early part of her life must have been. Not many people would have guessed that such a badly injured dolphin would one day return to full health—which makes Winter's story a very special tale about a very special tail.

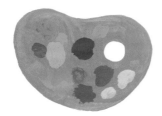

CONGO

The chimpanzee who became an artist

A BRIGHT IDEA

In June 2005 there was an unforgettable day in the art world. At a famous artwork auction in London, lots of people wanted to buy the same group of paintings by an artist who had died 40 years earlier. The person who eventually bought them spent a whopping $17,825, but there was something about these paintings that made them very unusual. The artworks were bright, bold, and colorful, which was normal enough, but the artist who created them had been much smaller and hairier than most painters.

Congo the chimpanzee loved creating works of art.

Congo the chimpanzee was born in 1954. He lived at London Zoo, and like many zoo animals, he led a life that was different than normal. At just a few years old, he appeared regularly on a television program called *Zoo Time*, which helped to teach children about the animal world. The host of the program was a man named Desmond Morris, who as well as being an animal expert was also an artist. It wasn't long before Desmond had an idea.

> **❝** *Congo could draw a circle and had a basic sense of composition . . . his favourite design was a sort of radiating fan pattern.* **❞**
> — The Daily Telegraph

PAINTING PICTURES

Like all young chimps, Congo was active and curious. He was also very intelligent, so when Desmond handed him a pencil and a piece of card, Congo soon realized that he could use it to make lines and messy patterns. He held the pencil in almost the same way as a human would. He seemed to enjoy it too, so Desmond began giving him a pencil more often. Sometimes Congo drew shapes that looked like circles. At other times, he made simple pictures that were very strange and scribbly but seemed to be done with care—a bit like a toddler might do.

The art world went wild for the paintings that Congo produced, each one selling for thousands of dollars.

Things got even more interesting when Desmond gave him paints and brushes. With more colors to choose from, Congo made paintings that were full of thick lines and splotches, often in a fan pattern. He very rarely went over the edges of the paper. The paintings were sometimes quite pretty, but what Desmond found most interesting of all was that Congo seemed to decide when a painting was finished. If Desmond tried to take it away before it was completed, the chimp would get upset. But when Congo didn't want to add any more to a painting—even if it was a very basic one—he could never be persuaded to continue.

> **66** *It is the work of these apes, not that of prehistoric cave artists, that can truly be said to represent the birth of art.* **99**
> —Desmond Morris, zoologist and TV host

MAKING HISTORY

People were astonished when they heard about Congo and his paintings. One art gallery in London was so impressed that in 1957 they held a special exhibition of his artworks—Congo was still only two or three years old! World-famous artists like Pablo Picasso, Salvador Dalí, and Joan Miró were all amazed by the chimpanzee. Picasso and Miró even put up some of Congo's paintings in their own studios.

Many decades later, Congo's story is still an extraordinary one. He lived for only ten years and never had the chance to swing through the jungle, but he taught us a very valuable lesson about how clever and creative chimpanzees can be.

GREYFRIARS BOBBY

A SPECIAL STORY

The Scottish city of Edinburgh is a magical place. It's full of sloping streets, hidden alleys, and rocky hills. The buildings are tall and their stones are as gray as thunderclouds. But among the jumble of houses and people, there's something surprising to be found. On an old street near the city center, there stands a small statue of a dog, sitting up alertly and staring into the distance. This is Greyfriars Bobby, a little dog who showed a huge amount of loyalty.

There are many stories about Bobby's life, and because he lived a long time ago, we don't know which of them are completely true. What we do know is that he was a Skye terrier, a handsome Scottish breed with perky ears, a short tail, and a thick, hairy coat. But today people remember him for more than just his good looks. The legend of Greyfriars Bobby is a very special one—and it begins more than 160 years ago.

MAN'S BEST FRIEND

According to the tale, it was 1856 when an old man named John Gray decided he needed a dog. John, who was known as Auld Jock by all his friends, worked as a night watchman for the Edinburgh police. His job was to walk the city's cobbled streets at night to check that no one was causing trouble. It could sometimes be dangerous, so having a dog to help him would be very useful. Soon he took on a six-month-old Skye terrier puppy, which he named Bobby.

At night, Auld Jock and Bobby patrolled the Old Town together, from the castle at the top of the hill to the bridge at the bottom. And every afternoon, when the castle gun boomed out to let people know it was one o'clock, the two of them would go to the same restaurant for lunch. Wherever Auld Jock went, Bobby would follow.

Bobby's gravestone reads:

GREYFRIARS BOBBY
DIED 14TH JANUARY 1872
AGED 16 YEARS

LET HIS LOYALTY
& DEVOTION
BE A LESSON
TO US ALL.

> **" ... there he continued to live, beside his first and only master, for 14 years, looked after and fed by kind neighbors and local children, until he died in 1872. "**
> —*The Independent*

But then came a freezing cold winter, and the old man became very ill. He died in February 1858, with Bobby by his side. Auld Jock was buried in Greyfriars Kirkyard, a graveyard in the middle of Edinburgh. But the day after his funeral, something strange happened. When the graveyard caretaker arrived the next morning, he found Bobby sitting patiently by Auld Jock's grave. The same thing happened the next day, and the next.

Every day—in sun, rain, or snow—
Bobby sat next to Auld Jock's grave. Whenever he heard the one o'clock castle gun, he would scamper off to the same restaurant that he and Auld Jock used to visit together. The people who worked there knew who Bobby was, so they made sure he was always given a meal. But the rest of the time, month after month, year after year, Bobby stayed in his spot in the graveyard.

MAKING HISTORY

The news spread about this devoted little dog, and he became very well known. People looked after Bobby, by bringing him treats and building him a shelter. Some even tried to give him a new home, away from Greyfriars Kirkyard, but Bobby always returned. He wanted to be next to Auld Jock. Amazingly, he spent 14 whole years waiting by his owner's grave, and when he died himself in 1872, aged 16, he was buried in the very same graveyard, close to Auld Jock.

One year later, a statue was put up nearby, and the legend of Bobby's life has grown even stronger over the years. He has had books written about him and was even the subject of a Disney film. Today Bobby's collar and drinking bowl have their own display at the Museum of Edinburgh and people still leave sticks and toys at his grave, remembering a dog who lived a quiet life—but who was a very, very faithful friend.

Bobby's statue in Edinburgh, Scotland, has a very shiny nose because thousands of people have rubbed it for luck.

87

KEIKO

The orca who lived an extraordinary life

A DIFFICULT BEGINNING

This is a big story about a big animal. It begins in the late 1970s, when a two-year-old whale calf was caught in the North Atlantic Ocean. It was a male orca, or killer whale, and he was taken to live in an aquarium in Iceland. For an animal as large as an orca, which normally lives in the sea, this is never a good thing. But for this young creature, it was just the first of many journeys he would make.

The orca's name was Keiko, which means "lucky one" in Japanese. After four years in Iceland, he was sold to an amusement park in Canada, where he spent the next three years having to perform tricks for visitors. The conditions here were bad for Keiko, and he became unwell. Unfortunately, his next home was no better. In 1985 he was bought by another amusement park, this time in Mexico, where he lived in a pool that was too shallow and too warm for him. He had problems with his skin, and he never saw any other orcas.

FAME AND FREEDOM

Then, several years later, something unexpected happened. A group of filmmakers in Hollywood wanted to make a film about an orca living in an amusement park who is set free. They needed an orca for the starring role—and after finding him in Mexico, the filmmakers chose Keiko to be that orca. The film was called *Free Willy*, and it was a worldwide hit. Millions of people went to the cinema to watch it—Keiko had become a film star.

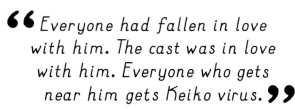

> **"**Everyone had fallen in love with him. The cast was in love with him. Everyone who gets near him gets Keiko virus.**"**
> —David Phillips, from the Earth Island Institute

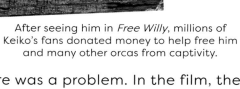

After seeing him in *Free Willy*, millions of Keiko's fans donated money to help free him and many other orcas from captivity.

But there was a problem. In the film, the orca escapes to freedom. In real life, Keiko was still in his small pool in Mexico. He was now 21 feet long and weighed three tons—and living in the pool was making him unwell. Lots of people around the world thought it was very wrong that Keiko was still living like this.

They said he should be released into the sea, and many children and adults raised money to help him. Eventually, Keiko was moved. But because he had spent so long in amusement parks and aquariums, it would have been too much of a shock to put him straight back into the sea. Instead, in 1996, he was flown on a special plane to a brand-new seawater tank in Oregon, where people got so excited by his arrival that the newspapers started writing about "Keikomania"! In his new tank, he could swim in salt water and learn to catch live fish again. It was the first time he had lived in seawater for 14 years, and he became healthier. Two years later he was flown again, this time to a big underwater net the size of a soccer field, in the sea near Iceland. He still wasn't completely free, but he was back in the waters where he had grown up.

Over the next few years, he sometimes left his net in the bay to swim in the open ocean. Finally, in 2002, he swam away for good, following a pod of wild orcas into the deep sea. We know that he traveled as far as Norway, where people spotted him close to the shore. But he was so tame that he still let humans come close enough to touch him. Poor Keiko wasn't ready to be an ocean orca. He found it difficult to live like the other orcas, because he wasn't used to being wild.

> **❝** *After his appearance in Free Willy . . . more than a million people wrote to demand that Keiko be set free. A huge global fund-raising campaign was set up.* **❞**
> — The Guardian

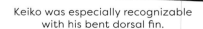

Keiko was especially recognizable with his bent dorsal fin.

MAKING HISTORY

When he died the following year, the world remembered a magnificent creature who had never been able to choose how he wanted to live. The better news is that because of Keiko's story, many more of us now understand that keeping orcas in amusement parks isn't fair to them. Keiko was an animal who touched the hearts of millions—and also helped to make the future better for other orcas.

WINNIPEG

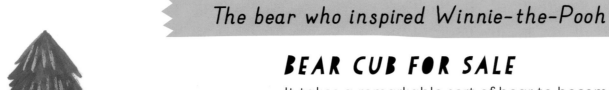
The bear who inspired Winnie-the-Pooh

BEAR CUB FOR SALE

It takes a remarkable sort of bear to become well known around the world. This is especially true for bears that are fictional, or made up. Most children know who Paddington and Baloo are, but there's one fictional bear who may just be the most famous of all. He's tubby, he's yellow, and he eats rather a lot of honey. His name, of course, is Winnie-the-Pooh—but did you know that the character wouldn't exist if it wasn't for one real bear that lived more than 100 years ago?

This bear's story starts on one continent and ends on another. It was August 24, 1914, just after the start of the First World War, when a Canadian soldier paid 20 dollars to buy a young black bear cub from a hunter at a train station. The soldier's name was Harry Colebourn, and he was on his way to an army base in Québec, eastern Canada, to join the Veterinary Corps—a group of soldiers that looked after army animals. Harry named the bear after his hometown: Winnipeg, or Winnie for short.

SEPARATED BY WAR

Winnipeg was a bear with a lot of character, and she quickly settled into life on the base. She tried to climb tent poles, slept under Harry's bed, and was fed on apples, milk, and corn syrup. She became very popular with the soldiers, so when they had to sail across the Atlantic to England two months later, Harry took Winnipeg with him. She was growing fast, and when they arrived, she followed the soldiers around their new base like a devoted puppy.

Then the Canadian soldiers had to travel to the battlefields of France. This would have been far too dangerous for a tame bear like Winnipeg, so in December 1914 Harry took her to be looked after at London Zoo. He was very fond of young Winnipeg and planned to take her back with him to Canada after the war.

> **"** *Winnie was quite the tamest and best behaved bear we have ever had at the zoo.* **"**
> —Ernest Sceales, a keeper at London Zoo

But the war raged on for years. Harry visited Winnipeg whenever he returned from France and he could see that she had become a favorite with visitors to the zoo. Incredibly, she was so gentle that children were allowed into her cage to pat and feed her! When the war finally ended, Harry's mind was made up. He was sad to say goodbye, but when he sailed to Canada, he decided to leave Winnipeg at the zoo.

MAKING HISTORY

The big, furry bear continued to attract lots of visitors. One boy in particular came to feed her again and again. The boy's name was Christopher Robin Milne, and his father was a writer named A. A. Milne. Christopher adored the bear so much that he gave his own teddy a new name, combining Winnipeg with the name of a friend's pet swan he also liked to feed, called Pooh. So alongside the other toys in Christopher's bedroom—which had names like Piglet and Eeyore—there was now Winnie-the-Pooh.

When Christopher's father began writing books about a lovable bear and his friends, it was obvious to him which names to choose. Since the first story came out in 1926, the Winnie-the-Pooh books have sold millions of copies. The real Winnie spent the rest of her life in the zoo, and she is remembered today with two statues: one in London, England, and one in Winnipeg, Canada. She even had a Hollywood film made about her life. Winnipeg was a very friendly animal who was surprisingly sweet-natured for her size—and in many ways, her story is just as memorable as the honey-loving yellow bear who took her name.

> **"** *The Winnie-the-Pooh stories would not have existed without Harry Colebourn and the decisions he made regarding his bear, Winnie.* **"**
> —M. A. Appleby, the author of *Winnie the Bear*

Christopher Robin with his bear, named after Winnie (*above*), and one of the Winnie-the-Pooh books (*left*).

KAMUNYAK

The lion who adopted baby antelopes

WILDS OF AFRICA

On the hot, golden savannahs of East Africa, animals have to do what they can to survive. When lions and antelopes spot each other, two things normally happen: the lions try to hunt the antelopes, and the antelopes try to run as far away from danger as possible. So when a lioness in Kenya found a young oryx, a type of antelope, and started looking after it as if it were her own cub, no one had ever seen anything like it.

The rolling wilderness of Kenya's Samburu National Reserve is home to all sorts of incredible African animals, from leopards and cheetahs to giraffes and zebras. The reserve also has lots of lions and antelopes, and it was here, in 2002, that people started to see something amazing: a lioness walking side by side with a baby antelope. What made it so special was that the lioness wasn't trying to eat or chase the skinny calf—she was trying to protect it.

As well as lions, the Samburu National Reserve is also home to many herds of elephants.

UNLIKELY FRIENDSHIP

Local people named the lioness Kamunyak, which means "the blessed one." She was only around three years old, but she was almost fully grown. The antelope was tiny and just a few weeks old, with wobbly legs and small horns. The two of them went everywhere together, striding across the plains, walking through the bush, even lying next to each other in the shade. Lions can be aggressive and very powerful, but Kamunyak was gentle with the calf, keeping it close at all times and letting it nibble her ears. People described it as a miracle.

66 *When she came across this baby oryx, instead of seeing 'food,' she saw 'baby.'* **99**
—Saba Douglas-Hamilton, a conservationist

> **"** *Nature is full of surprises. The story of a lioness adopting an antelope is the stuff of fairy tales.* **"**
> —Saba Douglas-Hamilton

AMUR & TIMUR

The story of Kamunyak and the baby oryx is a very odd one—but other animals have shocked us like this too. In late 2015, in a snowy safari park in Russia, a goat named Timur was put into the enclosure of a tiger named Amur, to give the tiger something to eat. But rather than kill the goat, Amur decided to let it live. Soon the two of them spent their days walking together, playing, and sleeping side by side!

> **"** *The goat showed his braveness and the tiger said, 'Okay, I respect that, let's be friends.'* **"**
> —Dmitry Mezentsev, the director of Primorye Safari Park

OWEN & MZEE

Kenya has another unlikely story—one that is perhaps the strangest friendship of all. Owen was a baby hippo who was rescued after being found all alone near the ocean. He was taken to a wildlife sanctuary, where he met a 100-year-old giant tortoise named Mzee. To everyone's surprise, the two formed a very close bond. Owen went everywhere with Mzee, sleeping with him, eating with him, and even licking his face!

Wildlife experts think that Kamunyak was acting like this because she had become separated from the rest of her pride, or lion group. She was all alone and needed some company. But because she wasn't the calf's real mother, she had no milk to feed it, and the little calf became very weak. Kamunyak made sure no other big cats attacked the young antelope, but she was getting hungry too. Then, after two long weeks, while the lioness and the calf were drinking water from a river, an adult lion sprang out from the bush and killed the poor calf.

MAKING HISTORY

What happened after this was even more surprising. Over the next few months, Kamunyak caught five more baby antelopes, looking after each one and staying close to them to make sure they couldn't escape back to their families. Experts have still never seen another lioness behave like this. She couldn't care for them as well as their mothers would have done, and the antelope calves would have been very confused, but Kamunyak showed us that in the wild, animals really can do the most unbelievable things.

HOOVER

The seal who could "talk"

SEAL ON THE SHORE

When an American fisherman named George Swallow saw a little seal pup alone on the New England coastline in May 1971, he knew that he had to do something. The baby was orphaned, with no older seals to look after him, and if he was left where he was, it would be very difficult for him to survive.

So George did something remarkable: he decided to take the pup to his house and care for him there, letting him live in the bathtub and feeding him fish. The seal gobbled up mackerel so quickly that he reminded George of a vacuum cleaner! This is how he was given his name—Hoover—and soon the animal grew far too big to stay in a bath. George moved him to a small pond outside (much to the delight of local children), but before long he was too large for this, too!

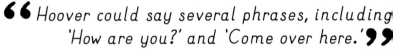

> **"** *Hoover could say several phrases, including 'How are you?' and 'Come over here.'* **"**
> —New England Aquarium in Boston

This was a very unusual way for a seal to begin life. Hoover's story, however, was only just starting. George took the fast-growing pup to the New England Aquarium, which was already looking after a group of seals. The helpers at the aquarium were happy to have a new seal, but when George told them something he'd noticed—that Hoover sometimes copied the words people said—they looked at George like he was crazy. Whoever heard of a talking seal?

George with Hoover at his new home in the New England Aquarium in Boston.

UNBELIEVABLE SOUNDS

It wasn't until a few years later that they realized George was telling the truth. Like the other seals, Hoover spent his days swimming, resting, and eating herring. And like the other seals, he barked and honked. But after a while, Hoover started making other noises too—noises that sounded exactly like a deep human voice. The helpers couldn't believe their ears. Can you imagine what a shock they got when they suddenly heard the words, "Hello there! Hey, hey, hey!" or, "Hoover, come on, come on!" echoing out of the seal enclosure?

> "He's the only talking seal in the world and the first non-human mammal ever to have produced these sounds."
> — The New Yorker

It was absolutely extraordinary. Not only was Hoover making noises that sounded just like words, they were also in a New England accent! Sometimes the seal would make the noise, "Come over here!" At other times it would be, "Get outta here!" Sometimes he would even make the two noises together—"Come over here! Get outta here!"—then give a big, loud laugh.

MAKING HISTORY

News of the seal's amazing ability spread fast, and thousands of visitors came to listen for themselves. Hoover appeared on the radio, in magazines, and on television. It was the first time anyone had heard of a seal who could mimic a human voice. Things got even more interesting when they realized that Hoover sounded exactly like George, the man who had helped him when he was a pup. Some people thought that because Hoover had heard George's voice so much at a young age, he had learned how to copy it!

Hoover cooling down on an ice block during a heat wave.

Just like humans, seals are mammals. They have body hair and feed on milk when they're babies. Their vocal cords—the folds of skin in their throat that let them make noises—are similar to ours too. This is how Hoover was able to do what he did. By the time he died in 1985, he had been a father to six pups. They were all beautiful animals, with big eyes and whiskery noses, but none of them could make the incredible noises their father could. It proved one thing: that there might never be another seal quite like Hoover.

SEABISCUIT

STARTING SLOWLY

This is the story of a racehorse that never gave up. Most racehorses are tall and graceful, but Seabiscuit was different. He was smaller than normal, with knobbly knees that didn't straighten properly. He had a sad little tail, ate too much hay, and slept more than he should have. Most people who saw him thought he was too short to be a proper runner. What they didn't know was that they were looking at a horse that would become one of the greatest of all time.

Seabiscuit was born in 1933 in Kentucky. His father was a racehorse named Hard Tack, which is a kind of biscuit that sailors eat. This is how Seabiscuit got his unusual name—and it wasn't the only thing about him that was unusual. As he grew up and began to race on the track, his galloping was so awkward that he lost his first 17 races.

Soon, however, things changed. Seabiscuit might not have been big, but he was fast. He started to win races, and a man named Charles Howard noticed how much energy the horse had. He saw something special in Seabiscuit, and before long he became his owner.

Charles's favorite picture of Seabiscuit, labeled with his unusual measurements.

FINDING HIS FEET

Most people thought Charles was silly to buy such a small racehorse, but there were two men who didn't: Tom Smith, a horse trainer, and Red Pollard, a jockey who was blind in one eye. Working together, they helped Seabiscuit get even faster. Tom treated him with care, fed him carrots, and even found him three animal companions to stop him feeling lonely: a stray dog, a pony, and a monkey! Meanwhile, Red started riding Seabiscuit in bigger races, and time after time, they crossed the finish line in first place.

People weren't laughing at Seabiscuit anymore. In fact, the horse was becoming more popular by the day. It was a very difficult time in America, with lots of people struggling to earn money, so they loved seeing Seabiscuit beating the taller, stronger horses. He became the horse that millions of ordinary people could cheer for.

Then Red had an accident and broke his shoulder. Seabiscuit had a huge race coming up against a much more powerful horse named War Admiral. Red was too injured to ride, but with a new jockey in the saddle, around 40 million people listened on the radio to hear Seabiscuit thunder around the track ahead of War Admiral. He won! The little horse from Kentucky was a national hero.

MAKING HISTORY

Seabiscuit was named American Horse of the Year for 1938 and had more newspaper articles written about him than any politician or film star. But his story wasn't over. Two years later Red and Seabiscuit were riding together again. Charles, Tom, and Red decided to enter him into the one big race that Seabiscuit had never won: the Santa Anita Handicap in California.

> 66 *Seabiscuit was nothing short of a cultural icon in America . . . as many as 40,000 fans mobbed tracks just to watch his workouts.* 99
>
> —from the book *Seabiscuit*, by Laura Hillenbrand

Seabiscuit winning the 1940 Santa Anita Handicap with Red Pollard (*above*), and a Seabiscuit toy from Bay Meadows Racecourse (*left*).

The experts thought Seabiscuit was past his best—but Red knew differently. In the stands, 75,000 people were shouting the horse's name. Seabiscuit started slowly but found his speed at the perfect time. With his hooves pounding the track, he moved up to third place, then second, then took the lead. When he crossed the finish line as the winner, he became not just a champion but a sporting legend: the stubby-legged racehorse who had won it all.

He had a bestselling book written about his life, and in 2003 his story was turned into a Hollywood film. Today a statue of Seabiscuit still stands at Santa Anita racetrack, remembering a horse who brought happiness to millions of people.

HONK 4 HAWKS!

PALE MALE
The red-tailed hawk of New York

HOME IN THE BIG CITY

New York City is always full of life. It's colorful, energetic, and exciting. The streets are crowded with people, the trains run 24 hours a day, and the buildings tower high into the sky.

You might think that a city like this wouldn't be home to many wild animals—but you'd be wrong. In its parks and trees, you'll find everything from raccoons and woodpeckers to squirrels and owls. Meanwhile, close to the famous Central Park, there's also a kind of bird that you would never normally find in a city. Red-tailed hawks are birds of prey, with hooked beaks, long, sharp claws, and broad wings, and until the early 1990s, no one had ever heard of a bird like this making its home on the New York skyline.

So when a young red-tailed hawk appeared one year—trying first to live in the park, then roosting at the top of a tall apartment building on Fifth Avenue—people were very surprised. The bird was a male, with light head feathers and a cream-colored underbelly. A local bird-watcher gave the city's new resident the perfect name: Pale Male.

FIFTH AVENUE FAMILY

It was so unusual for a red-tailed hawk to be roosting high above a busy street that the bird soon attracted wildlife lovers. Lots of people came with their binoculars to try and spot him soaring past the tower blocks. Pale Male seemed happy too—he had such a good view of the park from his roost that he could easily swoop down to catch squirrels and pigeons!

The next year Pale Male tried to start a family. The first hawk he paired up with was named First Love, but sadly she was hurt and had to be taken away to a special center for injured hawks. The second mate he found was a female named Chocolate, and together they built a nest 12 floors up on the side of a tower block.

By now, Pale Male and Chocolate were famous. Stories about them appeared in the newspapers and on television, and more and more people came to see them. It was a thrill to watch them glide over the city. Then, two years later, something very special happened—Pale Male and his mate hatched three eggs in their nest! Soon a whole family of red-tailed hawks could be seen flying over Fifth Avenue.

> **" *Bird-watchers have come from all over the world to catch a glimpse of the famous hawk and his mates.* "**
> —*New York Post*

For the city's bird-watchers, it was an astonishing sight—but the surprises kept on coming. When Chocolate died in an accident, another female appeared back in New York and paired up with Pale Male. Incredibly, it was First Love, now recovered from her injury. Together, she and Pale Male had five more hawk chicks.

MAKING HISTORY

As the years went on, Pale Male fathered more than 20 chicks from his roof-ledge nest, with different mothers coming and going. The people of New York loved seeing them all. In 2004, when someone removed the nest from the building because they thought it was making a mess, there was an uproar. Hundreds of people gathered in the park, shouting and chanting, to demand that Pale Male's nest be put back. So many people joined the protest that eventually the nest was returned.

Protesters demanding to have Pale Male's nest returned to the rooftop ledge.

Because Pale Male had so many chicks, who then had chicks themselves, there are now many other red-tailed hawk nests on the buildings near the park. New York is famous for many things, but the next time you think about the city, imagine the skies over Central Park, where even today, Pale Male's large family can sometimes be seen riding on the wind.

> **" *By all accounts, Pale Male is a great dad, teaching his little ones to fend for themselves in the big city.* "**
> —*New York Post*

TITUS
The gorilla king

MEETING THE GORILLAS

Sir David Attenborough makes wildlife documentaries about the world's most amazing animals and places, and his adventures have introduced us to wildlife from every part of the planet. He's been lucky enough to spot almost every creature you can think of, but the animals he once saw in East Africa were maybe the most extraordinary of all. Because in January 1978, deep in the thick green rain forest of Rwanda, Sir David came face-to-face with a troop of mountain gorillas.

> **"** He was a charming little animal. (Meeting him) was very memorable and I haven't been allowed to forget it. **"**
>
> —Sir David Attenborough, a naturalist and TV host

They were sitting in a forest clearing, relaxing on the ground and tearing off great fistfuls of leaves to eat. With their huge heads, shaggy black arms, and warm brown eyes, they were a breathtaking sight—and just as impressively, they stayed right where they were when Sir David approached. He crouched in front of them and started talking quietly to the camera, with a young gorilla sitting calmly right behind him. Nobody could have known it at the time, but this wild animal would go on to become one of the most famous gorillas that ever lived. His name was Titus.

LIVING WILD

The documentary gave us an incredible look at how gorillas behave. It showed them climbing, play-fighting, and resting—and at one point even wriggling around on top of Sir David! Titus was only a few years old when millions of television viewers first saw him on-screen, and his life was just beginning.

But he did not have an easy time growing up. All gorilla troops have a leader—usually a grown-up male called a silverback because of the gray hairs on its back—and when, tragically, hunters killed Titus's father and uncle, another male named Beetsme became the head of the gorilla troop. One of the first things the new leader did was chase away Titus's mother and sister.

Despite losing so many of his family members, Titus chose to stay with Beetsme's troop. He became a father for the first time at just nine or ten years old, younger than any other known gorilla—in fact, we now know he had at least 13 children! And by the time he became a silverback in 1991, he was ready to challenge Beetsme to become the leader of the troop. Titus was so strong and powerful that Beetsme couldn't stop him. The handsome little gorilla who had lost his parents was now the number one silverback.

> **"** *Titus's true gift to the world has been the amazing recorded history he left. He has provided an amazing picture of . . . mountain gorillas.* **"**
>
> —Sir David Attenborough

For the next 15 years, Titus led a troop of as many as 30 gorillas, which is much larger than normal. A team of experts kept a close watch on them during this time, so we know far more about Titus and his gorillas than we do about most wild animals. He was described as a happy and calm leader, who regularly took his troop up and down the steep mountains of the rain forest. He knew when to be quiet, when to be angry, and when to be caring.

Gorillas usually live in groups called "troops" made up of lots of females, their young, and one or more males, including a dominant silverback.

MAKING HISTORY

Titus appeared in many wildlife documentaries, even taking the starring role in one called *Titus: The Gorilla King*. People loved watching Titus on film, even in his final years, after one of his sons peacefully became the new leader of the troop. When he died in 2009, he was 35 years old and weighed 440 pounds, which is as heavy as two very large men. He was a gorilla who had a very sad start to life, but went on to become a great leader. And Sir David? Even all these years later, he still gets remembered for that magical moment in the heart of the African wilderness.

HACHIKŌ

The dog who spent years waiting for his owner

A NEW BEST FRIEND

Some people do things at exactly the same time every single day, like eating their breakfast or getting ready to go to bed. Routines can be just as important to animals as they are to humans, and one very faithful Japanese dog showed us just how true this is. The dog's name was Hachikō, and even though he lived almost 100 years ago, his story is still very special.

Hachikō was an Akita, a large and good-looking breed of dog with big ears, lots of fur, and a soft tail that curled up over his back. He was born in a part of Japan called Ōdate in November 1923, but he didn't stay there for long. At the start of the new year, the puppy was given to a man named Professor Ueno, who was a university science teacher in the busy capital city of Tokyo.

The two of them spent a lot of time together, and Professor Ueno quickly grew to love his new pet. It was clear that Hachikō was very attached to his new owner too. Every day, when Professor Ueno walked from his house to the station to catch the train to work, Hachikō walked with him. And every evening, when the professor returned home, Hachikō would be there waiting for him among the crowds at the station. Things went on like this for many months. The seasons changed, but Hachikō was always there to meet his master at the end of the day, in sunshine or in snow.

> **"** *Hachikō became renowned nationwide for his loyalty, praised in Japanese school textbooks and hailed in at least two major films.* **"**
> —*The New York Times*

DEVOTED DOG

Then, when Hachikō was nearly a year and a half old, something unexpected happened. Professor Ueno died one day while teaching at the university, and when the young dog went to the station to wait for him, no one came. Hachikō didn't understand why his master wasn't there. So he came again the next day, and the next. Eventually, someone who lived close by started looking after Hachikō, but every evening the dog still came back to the station, just as the train was arriving.

Night after night, as the noise and lights of the city swirled around him, he returned to the station. People started to notice the handsome Akita who was always there to meet the evening train. They would pat him and give him food. And when they discovered that he was waiting for an owner who had died many years earlier, the dog had an article written about him in a popular newspaper. All of a sudden, Hachikō became famous.

> **"** *The statue of Hachikō is an important treasure.* **"**
> —Kazuhiro Okuno, a Tokyo city development official

MAKING HISTORY

People across Japan were amazed by the dog's patience and loyalty. A statue was made in his honor, and Hachikō's story even started appearing in school textbooks so that children could learn the importance of being faithful. And still, every evening, he returned to the station to wait for Professor Ueno. People say that Hachikō waited for his owner every evening for nine years, nine months, and fifteen days.

Hachikō and Professor Ueno are forever reunited in a statue outside the University of Tokyo (above), and a Hollywood film named *Hachi: A Dog's Tale* was made about Hachikō's story (right).

When Hachikō died peacefully in March 1935, his legend lived on. A second statue of the dog was made, which still stands outside the station in Tokyo. Dog lovers hold a special ceremony there once a year to remember him, and there are shiny patches on the statue's legs where people have rubbed them for good luck. Today there are many other tributes to Hachikō around Japan, and in 2009 there was even a Hollywood film made about his life. Dogs are often called "man's best friend"— and dear, devoted Hachikō showed us exactly why.

SUDAN

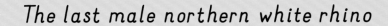

A LESSON IN CONSERVATION

There's no creature on the planet quite like a rhinoceros. With its huge horns, tough skin, and enormous body, it looks like an animal from the age of the dinosaurs. Rhinos aren't quite that old, but they have walked the earth for tens of millions of years. So when we hear about a type of rhino that has nearly disappeared completely, it's extremely alarming.

When a 45-year-old northern white rhino named Sudan died of old age in 2018, it was a very sad day. He was the last male of his kind anywhere in the world. There were just two females remaining, but without a living male it would be very difficult for them to ever have babies. It was a tragic way for Sudan's life to end—but his story also shows us just how vital it is that we look after the world's wildlife.

In 1975 a young northern white rhino living in Africa was captured by trappers working for a circus. Even back then, there were only a few hundred northern white rhinos left in the wild. The young rhino was bought by a zoo in the Czech Republic, where they named him Sudan, after the African country where he had been caught. His new life was very different from his old one—he was fed baked goods, visited by hundreds of people, and had to trudge around in the snow during winter.

> **"** *If we learn one thing from Sudan's passing, it should be that it's time for a new era of conservation.* **"**
> — *The Guardian*

Sudan spent almost 35 years living at the zoo. It would have been an unnatural life for him, although there were female northern white rhinos here too, so he was able to become a father to three rhino calves. One of them died very young, but his two daughters, Nabire and Najin, grew to become adults. In the year 2000, Najin even had a calf of her own, named Fatu.

GOING, GOING—GONE

However, though the northern white rhino population seemed to be doing well at the zoo, it was doing much worse in the wild. Hunters and soldiers had made it very difficult for the rhinos to survive, until in 2008 it was announced that there were none left at all. Tragically, the northern white rhino was now extinct in the wild.

By this time, Sudan was one of only four northern white rhinos left in the world. All of them lived in zoos. Experts thought that the best thing for the future would be to transport them all back to the plains of Africa, so in 2009, the four rhinos—two males and two females—were taken to a wildlife reserve in Kenya. Here, Sudan saw other kinds of rhino and learned to do things he had never done before, like sharpening his horn on a tree and wallowing in natural mud baths.

Sudan with his keepers at the Ol Pejeta Conservancy in Kenya.

MAKING HISTORY

The experts hoped that the males and females would produce more babies, but sadly, that never happened. The other male died in 2014, and as Sudan grew older and weaker, the chances of him becoming a father again became smaller and smaller. Wildlife lovers everywhere were shocked to hear that Sudan was now the last male in the world, and with his gentle nature, he became a symbol for the importance of conservation.

When he died, the two females that were left were Najin and Fatu, his daughter and granddaughter. Today they still live on the wildlife reserve, and scientists hope that one day they'll be able to help the females have babies. It would be very difficult—but if it worked, and the world had a chance to save northern white rhinos, it would be an amazing piece of good news.

> 66 *He was a gentle giant, his personality was just amazing and, given his size, a lot of people were afraid of him. But there was nothing mean about him.* 99

—Elodie Sampéré, from the Ol Pejeta Conservancy

WHERE THEY WERE BORN

1 Balto
USA

2 Koko
USA

3 Lobo
USA

4 Smokey
USA

5 Nim Chimpsky
USA

6 Binti Jua
USA

7 Seabiscuit
USA

8 Alex
USA

10 Hoover
USA

9 Winnipeg
Canada

11 Emily
USA

13 Roy & Silo
USA

12 Sergeant Stubby
USA

14 Pale Male
USA

18 Winter
USA

19 Lonesome George
Ecuador

20 Congo
England

21 Pickles
England

22 Christian
England

23 Streetcat Bob
England

15 William Windsor
England

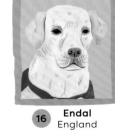
16 Endal
England

17 Cher Ami
France

24 Montaucie
France

25 Keiko
Iceland

26 Dolly
Scotland

27 Greyfriars Bobby
Scotland

28 Knut
Germany

29 Clever Hans
Germany

30 Hachikō
Japan

31 Trackr
Czech Republic

32 Duffy
Turkey

33 Laika
Russia

34 Wojtek
Iran

35 Simon
China

36 Moko
New Zealand

37 Lin Wang
Myanmar

38 Ozy
New Zealand

39 Huberta
South Africa

43 Sam
Australia

40 Jumbo
Sudan

41 Kamunyak
Kenya

42 Elsa
Kenya

44 Sudan
Sudan

45 Zarafa
Sudan

46 David Greybeard
Tanzania

47 Titus
Rwanda

48 Machli
India

49 Clara
India

50 Ning Nong
Thailand

GLOSSARY

9/11—A tragedy that took place in the United States on September 11, 2001, when airplanes crashed into New York's World Trade Center buildings. The numbers 9 and 11 stand for the month and day of the date.

ABATTOIR or SLAUGHTERHOUSE—A place where animals are taken to be killed, usually to be turned into food for humans.

ANTITOXIN—A kind of medicine that stops an illness or poison spreading through your body.

ANZAC DAY—A day held on April 25 every year to remember soldiers from Australia and New Zealand who died during wartime. "Anzac" stands for "Australian and New Zealand Army Corps."

AQUARIUM—A place where fish and other sea creatures are kept in tanks and enclosures, normally open to the public.

ARCTIC—The region above the Arctic Circle that surrounds the North Pole at the top of the world. It's usually very cold and icy.

ARTIFICIAL—Something made by people, often as a copy of something natural.

ARTILLERY—Big, powerful weapons that can fire over long distances.

ASTRONAUT—A spaceman or spacewoman.

BOY SCOUTS OF AMERICA—An organization in the United States that helps children to learn outdoor skills and other useful things. Despite the name, boys and girls can both join!

BUSKER—A person who plays music on the street to earn money.

CAPTIVITY—Being kept in a cage, tank, or enclosure. If an animal is in captivity, it doesn't live in the wild.

CENTRIFUGE—A circular machine that spins round and round very fast, creating a feeling like a rocket taking off.

CITIZEN—A person who lives in a certain region or place. For example, "He was a citizen of Taiwan."

CLIMATE CHANGE—The result of the man-made problems that are changing the planet's weather patterns.

CLONE—An exact copy.

CONSERVATION—The protection of nature and wildlife.

CONTINENT—A very large area of land, usually made up of many different countries. The world is made up of seven continents.

DIPHTHERIA—A disease. It affects the nose and throat and can be deadly if it's not treated.

DISPOSITION—A way of behaving. If you have a good disposition, it means you're kind and friendly.

DOCILE—Calm, gentle, and easy to look after.

EMBRYO—The tiny beginnings of a baby person or animal. An embryo grows inside the baby's mother.

ETHOLOGIST—A person who studies how animals behave.

EUCALYPTUS—A kind of tall tree common in Australia. It's also known as a gum tree.

EXTINCT—If a type of animal becomes extinct, it means there are no more of them alive anywhere.

FIFTH AVENUE—A long street in New York City, with lots of tall buildings and big shops.

FIRST WORLD WAR—One of the largest wars in history, taking place between 1914 and 1918 with armies from many different parts of the world.

FOUNDATION—An organization that helps raise money for a special cause, for example, the protection of animals.

GALLIPOLI CAMPAIGN—A fierce battle in the First World War, in what is now Turkey. Many soldiers died in the fighting.

GENIUS—Someone who is extremely clever and creative.

GOOD SAMARITAN—A person who does something very kind and thoughtful to help someone else.

GRENADE—A kind of bomb thrown by hand.

GULF WAR—A war that took place in different countries across the Middle East in 1990 and 1991.

HERITAGE—The special qualities of something from the past. If something has a heritage, it has a history and importance that is still strong today.

ICON—A person, animal, or thing that people see as heroic or very important.

INCUBATE—To sit on an egg and keep it warm, ready for hatching.

INSTITUTE—An organization that has been started for a special reason, for example, teaching a certain subject or studying a certain animal.

JOCKEY—A person who rides a horse in a race.

LABORATORY—A room or building where scientists work and do experiments.

LANCE CORPORAL—A rank in the British Army. It is the second-lowest of the army ranks, one above private and one below corporal.

LEGACY—The effect and influence that something has on the future. For example, the legacy of Lin Wang is that people now understand more about what makes elephants so special.

MAMMAL—Any animal with a backbone, hair or fur, and babies that feed on their mother's milk. Humans, cats, dogs, lions, tigers, and seals are all examples of mammals.

MARINE—To do with the sea.

MASCOT—A person or animal that is thought to bring good luck. Many sports teams and armies have mascots.

MIDDLE EAST—The region that includes the countries in and around Western Asia. It has big areas of desert, and the weather is usually dry and hot.

MILITARY—To do with the army, navy, or air force.

MUSHER—A person who drives a dog sled.

MUSTARD GAS—A poisonous and very dangerous gas that makes it difficult for people to breathe. It has been used as a weapon in some wars.

NATIVE—Of a place. If an animal is native to the United States, for example, this means that America is where the animal comes from.

NATURALIST—Someone who has a passion for wildlife and how the natural world works.

ORPHAN—A young person or animal whose parents have both died.

PENINSULA—An area of land attached to a larger landmass but mostly surrounded by water. Some peninsulas are small, others are very big. They can be narrow enough to walk across in a few minutes, or large enough to hold several countries.

PRIMATE—A highly intelligent mammal. Gorillas, monkeys, and chimpanzees (and humans!) are all primates.

PRIMATOLOGIST—A scientist who studies primates (see above).

PROGENY—The children of a human or animal.

PROSTHETIC—Artificial or man-made. For example, a prosthetic tail is one that has been made for an animal by humans, to do the job of a real tail.

RADIO TRANSMITTER—An electronic device that can send signals over a long distance.

SANCTUARY—A safe place. An animal sanctuary is somewhere where animals can live a quiet life away from danger.

SANTA ANITA HANDICAP—A famous horse race that takes place every March in the United States. It was first held in 1935.

SCIENCE FICTION—A type of storytelling, usually through books or films, which includes make-believe ideas about the future, space, or technology. *Star Wars* is an example of science fiction.

SCOTLAND YARD—A nickname for the offices of the Metropolitan Police Service, which is the police force for London, England.

SECOND WORLD WAR—The biggest and deadliest war the world has ever seen, involving more than 30 countries. It lasted from 1939 to 1945.

SIGN LANGUAGE—A way of saying things by using hand signs instead of speaking.

TIDAL WAVE or TSUNAMI—An enormous wave that causes flooding and damage to beaches and buildings, often started by an earthquake on the ocean floor.

VEGETARIAN—A person who doesn't eat meat or fish.

VICEROY—A ruler of a country or region, usually ruling on behalf of a king or queen.

WILDFIRE—A fierce fire that starts in the woods or countryside. It can spread very quickly and is often hard to control.

WILDLIFE RESERVE—A special area of protected land where wildlife can live naturally.

WORLD CUP—A soccer competition held every four years, where teams from several countries try to become world champions.

INDEX

PHOTO CREDITS
(Key: b-bottom; c-center; l-left; r-right; t-top)

CHAPTER EXPLANATIONS

RESCUE & PROTECT

Animals can sometimes find themselves in the middle of very dangerous and stressful situations. The animals in this chapter all reacted in amazing ways to what was going on around them. Some of them were caught up in wars, others in terrible disasters, but they all displayed incredible character. And they showed us that just as humans can look after animals, animals can look after humans, too.

ADVENTURE & EXPLORE

Many animals travel and explore, but the creatures in this chapter all made epic journeys that were out of the ordinary. Some of them had no choice about the voyages they went on, whereas others headed into the wild alone. But whether they traveled into outer space or roamed the African wilderness, they all did things that have become unforgettable.

CHANGE & SOLVE

Some animals lead such remarkable lives that they become famous around the world. This might be because they live to an astonishing age or become a symbol of conservation. It might be because they touch someone's life in such a special way that things are never the same for that person again. Whatever their stories, all the animals in this chapter deserve to be remembered forever.

DISCOVER & PIONEER

The more we understand about animals, the more we understand about the world around us. The animals in this chapter all helped us to see things differently. Many of them showed us behavior that we didn't think was possible or shaped the way that we looked at their species. And although the animals themselves didn't know it, they all made history.

INSPIRE & INFLUENCE

The animal kingdom is extraordinarily diverse, and the creatures in this chapter showed us just how impressive the natural world can be. From the sea to the sky and from the city to the jungle, they taught us that animals always have the ability to inspire and surprise us—and that our planet is a much richer place because of it.